EXECUTIVE ECONOMICS

EXECUTIVE ECONOMICS
Forecasting and Planning
for the Real World
of Business

WILLIAM J. HUDSON

JOHN WILEY & SONS, INC.

New York   •   Chichester   •   Brisbane   •   Toronto   •   Singapore

Copyright © 1993 by William J. Hudson
Published by John Wiley & Sons, Inc.

Library of Congress Cataloging-in-Publication Data:

Hudson, William J.
    Executive economics: forecasting and planning for the real world
  of business / by William J. Hudson.
      p. cm.
    Includes index.
    ISBN 0-471-56949-6 (cloth: acid-free paper)
    1. Managerial economics.   2. Corporate planning.   I. Title.
HD30.22.H83   1992   92-13549
330'.01'12—dc20

Contents

CONTENTS

PART ONE

*Trusting Yourself
Instead of
the Experts*

1

Who's in Charge of
Your Forecasts?

At all levels of a business organization, executives must be concerned with the present and future direction of the economy. Decisions about inventory, investment, and product development all hinge on the executives' outlook for economic growth. In a downturn, the byword is caution: Businesses concentrate on cost reduction and other strategies to hold market share against competition. In an upturn, however, the decision is whether to increase spending on plant capacity and new products.

The intimate relationship between the economy and business means that economic forecasting is a critical task for the executive. The more accurate a company's outlook, the better able it will be to compete and survive.

Do executives in general approach economic forecasting with the same ownership and zeal as their other competitive responsibilities? Or do they eagerly delegate the job of forecasting to "experts"? Does American business rely almost completely on professional economists for the key job of forecasting? If so, do the results justify the method?

Most readers will agree from their own experience that the forecasts of economists are notoriously wrong. The surprising thing is that, as business executives, we continue to tolerate such forecasts without searching for something better. Why haven't more executives simply concluded, "I can make better forecasts myself!"

ECONOMICS BY PROFESSIONALS—
AND THE ALTERNATIVE

The failure of executives to search for alternative approaches, or to dig deeply into the causes for the failure of economic forecasting, is all the more surprising in view of the current performance of American business. Haven't conditions become bad enough to drop all the politeness about grandiose credentials? Isn't it time to abandon methods that *should* work but do not? Isn't it time to pursue our bottom lines barefistedly? With our leading companies losing money and laying off millions of workers, shouldn't we be switching the emphasis from academically accepted approaches that do not work to more ruthless standards of whatever works best?

The persistence of the belief in professional economic forecasting, however, is amazing. After an outlook speech I gave in the summer of 1991, an executive for a Fortune 500 manufacturer came up to me to discuss the dilemma of his job as a division planning manager. "We rely on ABC Econometrics for our economic forecast," he said to me, naming a prestigious consulting firm on the East Coast. "They haven't been right for three years, but we keep making the same presentation to management." He then began to laugh, expecting that I would join in the amusement over this apparently insoluble problem. I told him that it reminded me of the old saying about Soviet workers pretending to work and the Soviet government pretending to pay them. In this American case, however, the staff pretends to forecast and management pretends to believe them. In many large companies we are paying top dollar for our economists. We regard them as the experts on the economy. Despite the fact that they are wrong, most executives believe nothing else can be done.

My questions to these companies are: Have you carefully tracked the forecasts of ABC versus the other available firms versus what really happened? Have you made your *own* forecasts, point by point, and compared these with the situation? The answer is almost always no.

I also ask: How right do forecasts have to be? How right *can* forecasts be? Don't we all know from common sense that no one can actually forecast the future? Shouldn't the goal of forecasting be if not actually to predict the future (which is impossible) then simply to come a little bit closer to the truth than the competition? Wouldn't achieving such a goal make a company relatively more efficient than its competitors and thus more profitable?

Then I ask: What has the staff of ABC Econometrics done to help you *understand* the economy better? What is the staff's relationship to your markets and your industry? Has ABC been able to give you powerful new ways to make better forecasts than your competitors?

The misplaced faith in economic experts and the sad performance of American business in the past decade are related in a more intimate fashion than most of us suspect. Most American executives have been *pretending* that they can understand their customers without having to understand the economy. The excuse has been that the economy is the proper and sole domain of economic experts, much the same way as engineering is the province of engineers. It is time to challenge this myth. The laws of economics are in no way comparable to the mechanical laws of motion. Human affairs do not behave in the manner of a spinning top or a large Swiss watch, yielding to simple predictions of periodicity. Human affairs, though not without a certain pattern, are much closer to chaos.

But because of the myth of economics as science, executives have been making a qualitative separation between *outlook* and *strategy*, and they have been focusing almost entirely on the latter. Executives have given away ownership of their own outlook. Outlook and strategy are virtually inseparable and business must take direct responsibility for both.

Whatever we mean by the "economy," and later we will come to this question mor exhaustively, it is surely something that enmeshes and influences every customer and every company. If today we preach the goal of knowing our *customer* better, how can this be done without knowing the *economy* better?

And if another principle of business improvement today is to give more power to first-line supervision—those in most direct contact with the customer and the market—how can we benefit fully unless the first line is also good at knowing the economy? The following must be considered:

1. The economy enmeshes us all, as executives and as customers. We cannot therefore turn the understanding

of the economy over to someone else and still expect to *know* our customers.

2. In terms of the academic discipline of economics, executives are amateurs. But in terms of company profits and the long-term survival of the firm, it is the amateur championship that matters, not the professional.

3. The executive's job is to beat the competition, using whatever works best, including the irreverent dismissal of experts who do not actually add value to the effort, regardless of their credentials.

4. The executive is often a much better amateur economist than our culture recognizes. A change in his or her attitude about what economics is, and about what to do with it, can often lead to dramatic personal growth and to much greater competitiveness for the company.

WE ARE ALL ECONOMISTS

An immediate objection to my views often comes directly from the chief executive officer: "I am not going to turn everyone in my company into amateur economists."

My reply is, "You don't need to; they already are." No businessperson who grows up in the United States, or in any other modern industrial democracy, can fail to be in some degree an economist.

The question is not whether all executives are amateur economists but what to do about it. Whether the chief executive officer (CEO) likes it or not, his job is to coach a team of amateurs and raise their level of play. The standard approach has been to dictate a single view of the economy from the top, as purchased from recognized experts at ABC or elsewhere, and then to expect the troops to march to this single tune. The face that the tune is usually off-key has been ignored. In view of the blatant failure of experts, why should it seem such an odd suggestion that a better tune could actually come from those doing the marching?

A loud objection, of course, comes from companies of economics experts like ABC, but this we would expect from any privileged class whose role in life we seek to devalue. A further objection from the CEO is, "I have no time for anything additional in my schedule, let alone to become a leading expert in economics."

My reply is, "Don't worry. In your company, you already *are* the leading expert in economics. You will do better if you *own* this responsibility rather than pretend you do not have it. Furthermore, you are not competing with professional economists but with other amateurs, other CEOs—the same ones you occasionally accuse of eating your lunch. Here's a chance to get some of it back. In all likelihood, they will continue to pay ABC Econometrics for bad outlooks."

The most stubborn barrier is *attitude*. In many cases, nothing I can say will change the determination of a firm to stay within the cultural norm—that is, to revere professional economists as though they were all Nobel scientists whose theories should work. A change of attitude is required to see economists merely as competitive knowledge workers, who should be held accountable for doing something that actually adds value to the firm. Until a company and its executives adopt the attitude about forecasting that it is a principal competitive task of the firm, it does no good to elaborate on the foundations and failures of economics. But once the attitude changes, and the appetite builds for beating the other guy at outlook as well as strategy, then the executive mind is hungry for new approaches.

This book is not another simplified explanation of the principles of economics. Instead it is an effort to trigger the adoption of a new attitude about the relationship between the executive and the economist. The book is meant to foster a new attitude about what economics is (and is not) and what business should do with economics. In its simplest form, the new relationship means that economists (and other kindred researchers) should not be paid for not being right (their wage would always be zero!) but for how much they help in making the willing executive slightly *more* right, *more* frequently, than the competition.

2

Is Economics a Science?

THE SCOPE OF ECONOMICS

The New Palgrave, A Dictionary of Economics,[1] published in 1987, supersedes the 1926 edition which in turn revised the original *Palgrave,* edited by R. H. Inglis Palgrave in the 1890s. *The New Palgrave* is 4,103 pages in four volumes. It includes 1,261 subject matter essays and 655 bibliographic essays, and represents the contributions of more than 900 authors, including the winners of 12 Nobel prizes in economics.

"One cannot do full justice to either the scope or depth of the essays without personally examining the entire works."[2] wrote Professor Dennis Henderson, in reviewing *The New Palgrave* for his colleagues in the Agricultural Economics Department at Ohio State University. "Herewithin I report on a selected sample of the essays," Henderson continues apologetically, confirming both the massiveness of the subject and yet the underlying presumption that no professional economist should speak with full authority until he or she has mastered every facet of the subject. (But who indeed can achieve this?) He goes on to say:

> Are you interested in revisiting a well-received economic concept or principle? In 10 minutes flat you can review Roy Green's essay on the classical theory of money, B. Lockwood's essay on Pareto efficiency, or Anwar Shaikh's essay of surplus value. Co-editor Milgate's essay on Keyne's General Theory will probably take a bit longer; better allocate closer to half an hour for Andrew Skinner on Adam Smith. Want something newer? Sunspot equilibrium is here, along with ARIMA models, negative income tax, rational expectations, and options pricing theory. Interested in competition? Entries range from atomistic competition (which, according to essayist A. P. Kirman would more appropriately be terms "atomless competition") to zero-profit condition, written by co-editor Eatwell. How about industrial organization? Essays range from administered prices to vertical integration. International trade will take you from autarky to vent for surplus. [3]

This should be enough, perhaps, to support the point with which I began my introduction. If the question is asked, "How can economics be explained by someone who is not an economist?" the answer is, "No one can explain economics who is not an economist. But of course, no economist can explain economics either."

ECONOMICS AS A BUSINESS RESOURCE

The point is that economics simplified is not really economics. Complexity is a crucial part of the discipline, a characteristic that economists themselves defend but that outsiders decry. Business executives, in particular, prefer analysis that is in 1-2-3 order, with clear conclusions. Economists, on the other hand, prefer uncertainty.

Purely in the interest of finding a way to gain some slim edge on our competition, suppose we wanted to explore the possibility of taking the "good parts" of economics and leaving the rest. Can this really be done? Is it possible to see economics as a vast intellectual resource—like history, mathematics, or physics—that expands the more you know about it but does not require mastering every detail before it becomes useful? My answer is, "yes," but but as an economist would say, "with certain important qualifications and cautions." Consider these three main points about economics as a business resource:

1. *Economics is an inescapable ideal.* As Plato observed long ago, we have never seen an absolutely perfect square or an absolutely perfect circle, but we *know* what they are. At a higher conceptual level, we have never witnessed perfect beauty or perfect justice either, but we know what they are. And so too, we have never witnessed perfectly rational behavior, but we know what it is. If such behavior were the norm on earth instead of the exception, then economics would be a perfect science. In the interim, however, economics (that is, rationality) not only serves as an ideal at which to aim our behavior but also as a framework of analysis that the human mind cannot ignore. The mind, in other words, may well recognize that the subject of its analysis (humans) is only partly rational, but this will not deter it from exercising the fullest possible logic—in the hopes of capturing at least partial truth and thus some measure of utility. Many principles of economics have this quality, that is, a measure of truth but not the full truth.

Caution. Many economists disagree with my views above. They believe instead that the analytic power of economics transcends the distinction between, say, reason and emotion, and that most of the things humans do with and to each other can be fully explained—including politics, marriage, and crime. We are all self-seeking individuals, rationally pursuing our own interests, and thus we are subject to the logical methods of microeconomics. "Of all the social sciences," writes Nobel prize winner George J. Stigler in his memoirs, "only economists possess a theoretical system to explain social behavior."[4] So the business executive shopping for sources of illumination and competitive advantage must travel en garde: The Platonic ideal of achieving "complete understanding" is waiting everywhere to spoil the search.

2. *Economics is an accepted tool of government policy.* There is no larger, more serious user of economics than government. This in itself justifies a better understanding of economics by business executives, for two reasons: to defend themselves against policies that may be seen to curtail business freedom, and to better foresee the likely course of government action and its impact on industries, markets, and customers. Government policies will always be proposed, debated, and launched in terms of selected economic principles, and they will be defended with economic statistics and projections. And in the international community, which is composed of dozens of separate but ever more comingling economies, officials have no real choice but to carry forward the debate on expanding the rules of commerce in terms of economic principles.

Caution. Important as it may seem to advocate a certain policy, for the benefit or preservation of a firm or an industry, the executive must make a clean separation between advocacy and outlook. The executive must distinguish between (1) the way he or she wants the world to be and (2) the way the world is. There is nothing wrong with trying to affect public policy, but there is great hazard in basing a company's economic outlook on the success of such advocacy. Absolute consistency, then, between the positions one advocates and the outlook one holds of future conditions will often be counterproductive.

3. *But economics is not an actual blueprint of human behavior.* If I were forced to define economics "rigorously," I might well focus on *The New Palgrave* as a kind of physical index of the underlying reality. My definition might be: Economics is a complex body of thought about human behavior, the standard dictionary of which consists of thousands of articles written by hundreds of authors—no single one of whom can be said to understand every important principle in detail. The interesting thing about the dictionary of economics, compared say with a dictionary of mathematics or physics, or even with the *Encyclopaedia Britannica*, is that many (if not most) professional economists hold out the prospect of reading, understanding, and connecting every entry. The most troublesome presumption we can all make as laypeople—referred to earlier as the myth of economics as a science—is to believe that all of the entrees in *Palgrave* are necessarily, logically linked. This leads to a wholesale replacement of verbal principles with algebraic formulas, and then to an enormous intellectual error called econometrics (about which I devote Chapter 4.)

Caution. The presence of contradictions (even so-called inherent contradictions) does not in itself destroy the value of economics, either in an ideal or a practical sense. A serious economist sees contradictions either as temporary gaps in understanding or as valuable points of view for highly complex situations. As noted by Henderson in his review, contradictions—such as the fact that one article refers to "atomistic competition" while another calls the same process "atomless"— are simply made into additional entrees in *Palgrave*. The same goes for the dozens of elegant denials of the foundations of economics—they become "grist for the mill," additional entrees in *Palgrave*. It isn't possible to do bodily harm to economics with logical analysis; the discipline absorbs such attacks as adding richness.

In my view economics is an inescapable ideal, an approach the mind automatically takes to the analysis of human behavior. Furthermore, economics is an accepted tool of government policy, which means that executives must rely on their knowledge of the discipline in order to defend themselves against bad policy and in order to foresee governmental impacts on markets. But economics is not an actual blueprint of human behavior. As a discipline, it is complex and full of contradictions—but resistant to logical attack.

The only opening is for a change in the executive's attitude about what the discipline really is and what business can do with it. When this change occurs, the executive is free to take only what he or she wants from economics, and leave the rest. When the business mind accepts ownership of the competitive necessity of making better forecasts than competitors, and when the business mind fully acknowledges that economics is not a perfected science but instead a limited toolbox, then—in a happy paradox—many of the parts of economics are much more valuable than the whole.

3

Failures of Forecasting

Despite the fact that most of us cannot remember ever having heard an economic forecast that was correct, the habit of mind in American business is to assume that correct forecasts do indeed exist, at least somewhere—perhaps in large international agencies, or at the headquarters of the Federal Reserve Board, or in the economic research units of big Wall Street banks. But alas, although the demand for accurate forecasts is acute, the supply is nil. The belief that someone, somewhere knows the future better than we do is a myth.

CAN THE IMF ACCURATELY
FORECAST WORLD GNP?

The International Monetary Fund (IMF), the agency that after World War II was charged with trying to balance accounts between all the world's countries, is one of the largest and most prestigious of all economic institutions. The IMF is the economic policeman for the world's banking system, holding debtor countries to tough reforms when they cannot meet their arrears. The IMF (together with the World Bank) has elegant headquarters in Washington, D.C., and pays higher salaries for professional economists than any other branch of government. But are the IMF's economic forecasts reliable enough to be used by business?

The Arithmetic of Large Numbers. Regardless of how good we may have been at math in school, we often have little appetite for number problems when we grow older. We usually skip over the numbers and pick up the story at the next point when we can see it returning to plain language and making sense to us. This tactic, however, often causes us to miss the main point in an argument about economics and to surrender ownership of the issue to "experts" (or at least to those who are willing to do the arithmetic, which might also happen to include our competitors).

Suppose, for instance, you are asked, "What is 1 percent of a billion dollars?" The answer is

$$\begin{array}{r} \$1,000,000,000 \\ \times\ 0.01 \\ \hline \$\quad 10,000,000 \end{array}$$

The next question is, "What is 1 percent of a trillion dollars?" This one is easy if you recall that a trillion is a thousand billion.

Just multiply the first answer, 10 million, by a thousand—giving you a figure of ten thousand million. Or, if the magnitude of these sums drives you to paper for reliability,

$$\begin{array}{r} \$1{,}000{,}000{,}000{,}000 \\ \times\ 0.01 \\ \hline \$\quad 10{,}000{,}000{,}000 \end{array}$$

The answer is $10 billion—a much larger sum than $10 million, for sure, enough perhaps to pay 20 percent of the cost of the Persian Gulf War in 1990–91.

The last question is, "What is 1 percent of $20 trillion?" We can all multiply 20 times $10 billion to get $200 billion, or roughly the size of the economy of Mexico.

The point of this short exercise in arithmetic is to build toward an insight about the size of the world economy and to comment on the record of that institution in whom we vest its surveillance, the IMF.

The size of the world economy in 1990 was about $20 trillion. The average growth rate in this aggregate over the past decade has been 3 percent. A 3 percent growth applied to $20 trillion would be $600 billion. A 2 percent growth, however, would be only $400 billion, or $200 billion less. Thus, when a forecast of world gross national product (GNP) is off by 1 percent, it is off by $200 billion, which is (once again) roughly the size of the economy of Mexico.

IMF's Track Record.   Examine Figure 3–1, which compares the IMF's forecast of growth in the world economy with its actual growth. Each spring, the IMF's staff of several hundred economists makes a forecast of world economic growth and gives its prescription for improvement. The forecast is contained

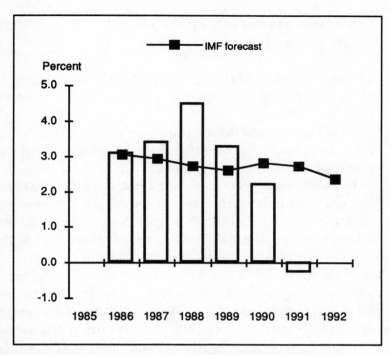

Figure 3-1. World GNP, 1986–1992, showing forecasts by the IMF.

Each May, the IMF forecasts world GNP for the current year and for the following year. But with the track record of these forecasts, should a business executive take them seriously? For instance, after missing the target so badly in 1990 and 1991, why would the IMF's accuracy improve for 1992?

(Source: IMF, World Economic Outlook, various issues.)

in a half-inch-thick report costing $60 per copy. Three errors in the forecast are significant:

1. The IMF has missed the direction of the change in world economic growth in three of the past six years, between 1986 and 1991.
2. The IMF has missed the magnitude of the change in world economic growth by more than $200 billion in three of the past four years, through 1991.
3. In the past seven years, through 1992, the IMF's forecast has changed only within the range of 3.4–2.9 percent, which means basically that in each year, whether they intend to or not, the staff simply predicts average growth.

Should Business Trust the Latest Forecast?   The forecast for 1992, had we been able to take it seriously during the preceding year, was astonishing. With 1991 at a sluggish 0.9 percent, the IMF said that in 1992 the growth in the world economy would return to nearly average, or 2.9 percent. In dollars, the 1992 increase would be about $400 billion, or altogether like adding another China to the whole pot. If the world economy were going to expand by $400 billion in 1992, should every business in the world have doubled and tripled its investment during 1991 to be prepared?

"Hey, we all know that economics is tricky," some readers may argue. "These people are doing the best they can and there's no point in ridiculing them for being off a percent or two."

Someone else might add, "I'd like to see you do any better!" and with such a person I would surely agree. The key factor in the period 1989 through 1991 was the political change in the Soviet Union. I personally had no idea that communism would begin to unravel in 1990—but apparently neither did the IMF (or the CIA [Central Intelligence Agency], the World Bank, the OECD [Organization for Economic Cooperation and Development], the G-7, the Congressional Budget Office, the Congress, the president, Harvard University, or anyone else). And in 1991 I had no trustworthy idea of how strong the world's economy would be in 1992, or whether the Soviet economy had reached bottom and would begin to grow again.

But I did have enough common sense to know that the IMF's forecast of a return to average growth in 1992 was indeed chancy. I took the irreverent position that the big team of IMF economists, with the world's most elaborate computer models, simply could not agree among themselves on any forecast that departed significantly from average.

CAN THE FED FORECAST A U.S. RECESSION?

Another institution with enormous prestige and with an undisputed degree of influence over the economy is the U.S. Federal Reserve Board. The Fed is the government's central bank, in charge of how rapidly to supply money to the economy to help assure economic growth while not enabling the rise of inflation. The mechanism used by the Fed is to increase or decrease the amount of money (actually checks drawn on the Fed itself) in the reserves of commercial banks, which in turn are more free or less free to lend these funds to the borrowing public, both companies and individuals.

The decision process about how much money to supply the economy includes an exhaustive amount of economic research, including the use of the world's most sophisticated models of U.S. GNP, interest rates, exchange rates, and money supply—

there are literally hundreds of different indicators to track. One special advantage that the Fed's governors have over other economic teams is the "live pulse": In each of twelve regions around the country, the president of the regional Fed has a board of governors to keep him or her informed about loan availability, prices, and orders. The twelve regional presidents bring this last-minute intelligence with them to Washington every six weeks, when the Fed's Open Market Committee (FOMC) meets to assess the condition of the economy and to issue a new directive to the New York Fed (the lead bank in creating money) about the degree of pressure appropriate for the country's bank reserves, and thus the level of interest rates. The Fed tightens these reserves when the economy is growing rapidly and when inflation is feared, and the Fed loosens the pressure on these reserves when the economy is facing a recession and inflation is in check.

As shown in Figure 3–2, the U.S. economy entered a recession during the third quarter of 1990. *Question:* With all the resources at the disposal of the Fed, was it able to forecast this recession before it happened? *Answer:* Read through the following log of public announcements by the Fed and its officials for July 1990 through December 1990 and then decide if and when such a forecast was made.

Fed's Statements About GNP Growth July–December 1990

> July 3, 1990. "The information reviewed at this meeting [of the Federal Reserve Board's Open Market Committee] suggests that *economic activity is continuing to expand* at a relatively slow pace."[1]
>
> July 18, 1990. "Things are not doing all that badly. The

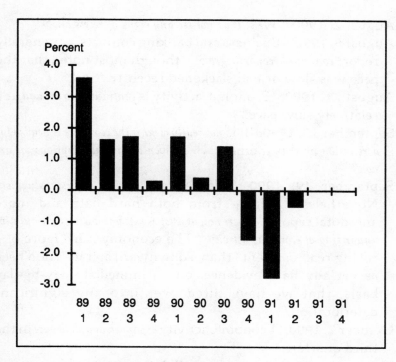

Figure 3-2. U.S. GNP by quarter, 1989–1991.

Some time during October–November 1990, growth of the U.S. economy stopped and receded. Did the Federal Reserve Board predict this recession before it happened? (The answer is no. For discussion, see pages 22–24.)

(Source: Joint Economic Committee, Economic Indicators, various issues.)

economy still appears to be growing and *the likelihood of a near-term recession seems low."* The Fed expects "somewhat sluggish" growth in the second half of the year.[2]

July 24, 1990. "We clearly have a sluggish economy." But *"the chances of a recession are low."*[3]

August 2, 1990. "*We still do not see any signs of recession.*"[4]

August 8, 1990. "Business and banking contacts . . . generally report *continued economic growth,* though most noted that the pace was slow or had slackened recently."[5]

August 21, 1990. "Economic activity is *continuing to expand* at a relatively slow pace."[6]

September 13, 1990. "It is *not really clear if the economy is headed for a recession* at this moment. . . . *Given certain assumptions we are not.*"[7]

September 19, 1990. "Clearly, *growth is, at best, sluggish.* Nonetheless, judging from both hard data and more anecdotal reports, *we are not, at least as yet, witnessing a cumulative unwinding of economic activity.*" The economy is in "more of a rolling readjustment" than a downward spiral. "I don't see as yet any hard evidence, on an immediate day-by-day basis, that we have tilted over into any significant deterioration."[8]

October 2, 1990. "Economic activity *expanded at a slow pace* in the third quarter."[9]

October 19, 1990. "Economic activity appears to have grown slowly in most Federal Reserve districts since early August, but seems to have declined somewhat in others."[10]

November 13, 1990. "The information reviewed at this meeting suggests a *weakening* of economic activity."[11]

November 28, 1990. "A *meaningful downturn* in aggregate output occurred" in October and November. "We won't know whether it is the beginning of a recession, or just some aberration, for quite a while. . . . We obviously are in a slowdown."[12]

December 18, 1990. "The information reviewed at this meeting suggests an *appreciable weakening* of economic activity."[13]

Sometime between early October and November, the growth rate of the U.S. economy, in aggregate, turned negative. According to its public statements and its actions, however, the Fed could not tell for sure that a recession was actually going to occur. Even in December, when the Fed believed that "an appreciable weakening" was underway, it was not really sure that the weakness would last long enough to fit the official definition of a *recession*, which is usually considered to be two consecutive quarters of negative growth. In other words, with all the tools at its command, and with a large professional staff monitoring events day-by-day, the Fed did not and could not forecast a recession in U.S. GNP.

The above log of the Fed's statements about GNP growth is stripped of all the normal camouflage accompanying the daily unfolding of economic news. For one thing, all of the key economic indicators are released but then revised, and usually revised again. It may appear to an observer in July that the economy is reported to have been positive through the previous June, but then in August the figure is revised to show that the economy was actually negative during the period (see Figure 3–3).

To be useful, indicators must be timely, but to be timely means that preliminary versions of the indicators must be estimated on the basis of incomplete information. When more and more information is received, the earlier sample of data may prove to be misleading. But to wait for complete information before issuing any indicators makes the indicators obsolete when they are finally released.

The argument that many economists make about data is probably true. "If we only had better data, our forecasts would be more accurate!" But collection of data on the activity of 250 million people is no small task and to expect that the quality of

Month of estimate	Percent growth for quarter					
	90-1	90-2	90-3	90-4	91-1	91-2
Jul-90	1.7	1.2				
Aug-90	1.7	1.2				
Sep-90	1.7	0.4				
Oct-90	1.7	0.4	1.8			
Nov-90	1.7	0.4	1.7			
Dec-90	1.7	0.4	1.4			
Jan-91	1.7	0.4	1.4	-2.1		
Feb-91	1.7	0.4	1.4	-2.0		
Mar-91	1.7	0.4	1.4	-1.6		
Apr-91	1.7	0.4	1.4	-1.6	-2.8	
May-91	1.7	0.4	1.4	-1.6	-2.6	
Jun-91	1.7	0.4	1.4	-1.6	-2.8	
Jul-91	1.7	0.4	1.4	-1.6	-2.8	0.4
Aug-91	1.7	0.4	1.4	-1.6	-2.8	-0.5

Figure 3-3. U.S. GNP growth by quarter, 1990–1991, showing revisions in the official estimates.

At the end of each three-month quarter, the U.S. Department of Commerce releases an estimate of the growth rate of the economy (the GNP). The first such estimate is preliminary, the second is revised, and the third is final. Note that the change between estimates from preliminary to revised to final can be substantial—for instance, the revised estimate for 1991–1992 changes from a positive growth of 0.4 percent to a negative figure of −0.5 percent. Not only GNP but most other economic indicators are subject to similar revisions. Even so-called final estimates can be revised on subsequent years.

(Source: Joint Economic Committee.)

data can eventually be better than at present is wishful thinking. Every day the economy is growing more and more complex and it becomes vastly more difficult to sample.

But the main problem that the Fed faced in forecasting economic activity during the autumn of 1990 was not the data revision problem. The problem was the appearance of three wild cards never before seen in the historical deck. The first of these was the Persian Gulf War, which spurred the price of crude oil to all-time record highs, adding to the fear of inflation. The second of these was the last-ditch drama of the Congressional Budget Accord of September–October 1990, which the Fed saw as crucial to holding down future inflation and to bringing down long-term interest rates. And the third was the so-called credit crunch, the name applied to the new unwillingness of banks—regardless of the plentitude of their reserves and the falling of interest rates—to actually loan money to anyone who did not have a flawless application.

Most observers say the credit crunch was the result of the easy lending practices of the 1980s that left many banks (especially the savings and loans) in collapse or in such weak positions that they could not afford the "normal" number of additional weak loans. The situation with the banks was so tenuous that the Fed appeared to spend as much time surveying loan standards and considering and making rule changes as it did on the overall economic outlook. As the recession in GNP began in October–November 1990, it earned the name of a *financial recession* rather than the usual *business cycle recession*.

The point for executives is, when do you expect to see the world's economic deck not have important wild cards, either financial, political, military, or other? Most will agree that the answer is "Never." Thus, does it make sense to adopt an economic outlook from the teams of experts whose methods make no adequate allowance for the unusual?

CONSENSUS FORECASTS OF PRIVATE ECONOMISTS

On September 20, 1990, the *Wall Street Journal* published the following forecast[14] provided by *Blue Chip Economic Indicators*, a monthly newsletter that surveys and then averages the forecasts of some fifty leading economists:

Quarter	GNP Growth Forecast	GNP Growth Actual
90−1		1.7%
90−2		0.4
90−3	1.0%	1.4
90−4	0.0	−1.6

The consensus for the last two quarters of 1990 was for a slowdown, but not for an actual recession of growth. Earlier, on August 13, 1990, the *Wall Street Journal* published a consensus outlook of some three dozen noted economists (some of which are also used by *Blue Chip*)[15] that predicted a 0.3 percent growth of GNP in the second half of 1990, followed by a 1.0 percent growth in the first half of 1991. Of the thirty-four economists in this August outlook, only six predicted a negative figure for GNP in the second half of 1990, and only two predicted negative figures for both the second half of 1990 and the first half of 1991 (which is the way it turned out). The two were Allen Sinai of the Boston Company, who called for −0.7 percent and −0.2 percent growth rate, and A. Gary Shilling of Shilling and Company, who called for −2.2 percent and −3.5 percent.

Hindsight gives the accuracy award to Shilling, but the question facing us now is the same as in the fall of 1990: How do we know which expert is right? (As a matter of fact, Shilling had been bearish on economic growth for quite some time and thus had a more dubious record before ringing this particular bell.)

In July 1991, *The Economist* decided to commence with its own consensus forecasts.[16] In discussing this decision, the editors said:

> How accurate are consensus forecasts? Robert Eggert, editor of *Blue Chip*, surveys roughly 50 American economists each month. Over the past 14 years the average GNP-growth forecast that the *Blue Chip* panel has made in October for the following year has had an average error (ignoring plus and minus signs) of 0.9 percentage points compared to the final outcome. This includes the worst year, 1982, when the consensus was for GNP to grow by 2.2 percent; it actually fell by 2.5 percent.

An average error of only 0.9 percent sounds very reassuring at first. But as shown in Figure 3–4, the *forecast range* for GNP growth is only from −3 percent to +7 percent, meaning that the *Blue Chip* error is actually a full 9 percent of the range. Furthermore, how can we ignore plus or minus signs? What if a business had relied totally on the 1982 forecast by *Blue Chip* of 2.2 percent growth, only to expand directly into a recession of *minus* 2.2 percent?

The same issue of *The Economist* describes research by the Fed,[17] who in humbler moments admits the need to improve forecasting by any means possible:

> Stephen McNees, an economist at the Federal Reserve Bank of Boston, has studied the accuracy of the 22 forecasters who have been on the *Blue Chip* panel since it was set up in 1977. He concludes that for a single variable, such as inflation, about a third of the

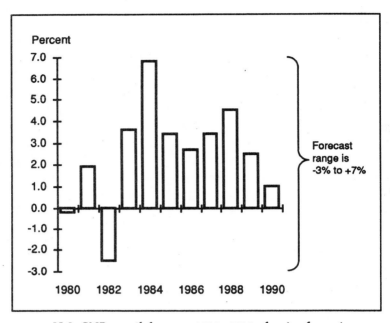

Figure 3-4. U.S. GNP growth by year, 1980–1990, showing forecast range.

In the past decade, and for most of its postwar history, U.S. GNP has varied between growth rates of −3 percent and +7 percent. Thus when a forecast of GNP is off by 1 percent of actual growth, it is off by 10 percent of the forecast range.)

(Source: Joint Economic Committee.)

forecasters are consistently more accurate than the consensus. But each forecaster has strengths and weaknesses. He may be an ace at forecasting GNP, but miss inflation by a mile. Although almost every forecaster can claim to be more accurate than the consensus for at least one variable, nobody beat it on all the seven indicators covered. Taking all the indicators together, the consensus forecast has had a smaller average error over time than all but five individual forecasters.

These findings confirm what we might well expect: It is not advisable to pick a single economic forecaster and trust him or her exclusively, as he or she will likely be worse on average than the consensus. But neither is it advisable to follow only the consensus, for it will be wrong by about 10 percent of the forecast range, on average, and it will occasionally miss the big changes in direction by a mile.

The reader of this book who adopts my own point of view will learn to accept the consensus as the consensus (that is, as simply what the majority believes), but will be prepared to make his or her own forecast independently and to take ownership of its accuracy against that of the competition's.

4

Economic Models Versus Economic Reality

Every year, sometime during October, announcements are made from Sweden of the year's winners of the Nobel prize. The categories include great achievements in chemistry, physics, medicine, literature, and peace—and, since 1968, economics. The Nobel prize in economics nowadays pays $1 million to the winner, to say nothing of the enormous prestige, which cannot be matched by any other award. A contest develops among journalists in the wire services and the big newspapers—the *New York Times*, the *Wall Street Journal*, the *Financial Times* of London, and others—to praise the winner's intellectual contribution and to interpret for the public exactly what the contribution was and how it fits in with the great achievements of economics in the past and with the events shaping history today.

As these stories on the Nobel prize in economics hit the front page, it is particularly hard for any reader, including the business executive, to distinguish between the fact that (1) economics as a discipline has unquestionable value for business and government and that (2) economic *forecasting* is virtually a complete failure. In an attempt to elucidate this distinction and then to move into a fuller explanation of the difficulties faced by econometric forecasting, let us consider briefly two of the prize winners, ten years apart, in 1981 and 1991. The most recent case is of a man who made us *think* about government, law, and business in fresh and powerful ways, whereas the earlier case is of a man who originated most of the techniques still used today in econometric modeling.

The 1991 prize winner was Ronald Coase, a professor of law at the University of Chicago. The Nobel committee recognized Coase for two main ideas: one concerning the role of transaction costs in business and markets, and the other concerning property rights and economic efficiency.[1]

Coase's idea about *transaction costs*—the costs of making transactions between people in organizations—was that they are often just as important as other more obvious costs, such as those of goods and services. In Coase's view, the emergence of very large corporations—for example, a McDonald's instead of ten thousand separate hamburger stands—occurs when such firms can provide a lower total transaction cost than what operators would have to pay individually. A large firm, by eliminating uncertainty and costly one-time negotiations through stable, contractual relationships among the members of the firm, achieves a cost advantage over competitors that is just as real as the more tangible advantages of scale, technology, raw material price, transportation cost, and so on.

Coase's idea about property rights and economics is sometimes called Coase's Theorem. The theorem states that the allocation of such legal entitlements as property rights has no bearing on economic efficiency if these rights can be freely traded. For instance, a government has two choices in attempting to reduce pollution from a given industry: (1) It can establish a minimum level of emission that each and every plant must attain, or (2) it can set such a level but allow companies above the level to buy pollution permits from other companies that have invested in being well below the government's regulatory level. Free trade in these legal entitlements to pollute will help to assure not only that the overall regulatory minimum is achieved but also that it is done in the most efficient manner.

A principal value of these ideas is to stimulate the executive's mind to examine the foundation of the competitiveness of his or her firm. For instance, the executive might think, "I wonder how low my transaction costs are compared to other firms in this industry"; or, "I wonder if there are some operations better done by small outside contractors because they will have lower transaction costs in particular areas"; or, "Does my company have technical advantages that could be traded to other companies in the form of pollution permits, thereby reducing our overall cost of doing business? What other things besides pollution are there to which I could apply this idea of trading property rights?"

Professor Coase is an excellent example of the economist as expositor-teacher to business and government, rather than as economic seer. "By forcing economists and lawyers to rethink the question [of property rights]," said Peter Passell in the *New York Times*, "Mr. Coase focused the attention of legal scholars on what it takes to make markets work efficiently without government to call balls and strikes.'[2] And furthermore, according to Michael Prowse in the *Financial Times*, "Professor Coase is also significant as one of a dying breed of economists who advanced their arguments in simple prose—rather than higher mathematics—and who believed economics should be relevant."[3]

But altogether the journalistic headlines surrounding the Nobel prize to Coase (or any of his forerunners) take us in a different, sensationalized direction: a "leap in theory," a "break-through in understanding the institutional structure of the economy," a "deflecting of economists from a research dead end," a "breathing of new life into the stagnant field of industrial organization," a "fundamental contribution which greatly added to the realism of economics theory," and an "explanation of why communist economies fail." The press coverage suggests an image of economics as a hard science, to which scholars are adding small bits of knowledge everyday that will soon coalesce into a single, grand, coherent theory.

We know, however, from an examination of *The New Palgrave* that the discipline is becoming ever more enormous, complex, open-ended, and contradictory. And we know from common sense that the forecasts of economists—whether those of the International Monetary Fund, the Federal Reserve Board, or large, prestigious (but money-losing) banks—are getting worse, not better.

Let us turn then to the branch of economics known as mathematical economics, or *econometrics*. In my view, the discipline has been discredited by the love affair that so many economists have had with extracting just the pure numbers from history and building these into algebraic models.

In 1981, the Nobel prize in economics went to Lawrence

Klein, then of Wharton Econometrics, for his contributions to the origins and development of econometrics. In fall 1981, I attended a symposium given by the Federal Reserve Bank of Kansas City on "Modeling Agriculture for Policy Analysis in the 1980s," at which Dr. Klein was scheduled to speak. His appearance at this secluded conference in Vail, Colorado, occurred only days after the Nobel prize had been announced, so there was a powerful aura of dignity around him wherever he went in the hotel. In his speech, he defined his mathematical models as "approximations of *reality.*" I was struggling to decide whether to continue using Klein's methods in the preparation of forecasts for the company at which I worked and in my notes I wrote two questions: (1) Isn't there more to reality and history than numerical indexes? (2) Is history, even in its broadest sense, a deterministic guide to the future?

At least one other speaker held the same skepticism as I did, a man who was then a policy aide at the White House. He approached Klein gingerly, not wanting to tackle the prestige of a Nobel laureate directly; rather than saying that econometrics doesn't work, he gave the audience a list of the reasons why modeling had not yet been more widely used by policymakers:

1. Policymakers must act in a way that leads to staying in office.
2. Time spans for policymakers (or any decision makers) are too short and are too much influenced by nearby situations to employ long-term models.
3. The path is as important as the destination. Attractive policies must also be achievable via tenable routes.
4. Who wins and who loses is a crucial aspect of American policymaking, and it is not covered by models.
5. Models have misplaced preciseness—it is better to be

moderately right in direction than attempt to be correct in magnitude.

6. There is a tidal-wave effect: Policymakers control very few variables and are easily swamped by things not within their control.

The difficulty with models of the keenest interest to me, then and now, was not mentioned by anyone at the conference in Vail—namely that business executives cannot relate to outlooks and strategies merely on the grounds that the model says it comes out that way. In other words, the models are so mathematically complex that even their authors, with or without a Nobel prize, cannot explain them in nonmathematical language, but can only keep repeating what the assumptions were and what the final printout says. This would be fine, perhaps, if the track record of the models was any good, but of course it is not.

Despite the poor track record and despite the explicit objections mentioned above in 1981, the decade of the 1980s became a heyday for econometric forecasting—not really losing luster until its closing years. How did the mathematical economists gain such a dedicated following and how do conditions differ today? And if what I say about the inaccuracy of economic forecasts is true, what are the specific flaws in economic forecasting that we must try to overcome by alternative methods?

ECONOMETRICS AND A CLOSED U.S. ECONOMY

In the immediate post–World War II years, a strong demand developed for economic advice, especially from government—

emanating from the "take command" approaches that were seen as having helped to win the war. At the same time, the amount of government-generated economic data increased and a new supply of researchers emerged to meet the demand for answers. "Experts" cropped up all over the country, most of them in the "hard" sciences (for example, physics, chemistry, mathematics). Practitioners of the newer "soft" sciences (including social science, political science, and economics) sought the same status as other experts. The transfer of quantitative methods to the soft sciences looked as though it would be fruitful and many bureaucrats already disposed to believe in central planning (as opposed to the "invisible hand") were intrigued. Maybe the day of rational control over human affairs was dawning!

The 1950s and 1960s provided economists with a nearly ideal period for successful forecasting: The country was at peace, it was as yet relatively unregulated (though the economists would themselves help to change that), and, above all, it was isolated from foreign economies by an effective monetary arrangement (the 1946 Bretton Woods agreement, which established fixed exchange rates) and by nearly absolute military hegemony. Terrorism was a local, not international, phenomenon, and Islamic rulers sat atop their enormous oil reserves, apparently quite content to accept a mere $1.80 per barrel, year after year.

Businesses began employing economists in great numbers to better coordinate their capital spending and inventory levels with the normal business cycles of the economy. Economists were seen as highly educated specialists to whom management assigned a specialized role on the business team. Their job was to provide an annual economic forecast on which the company's operating plan could be confidently based. For so many companies to establish and fill a new position called *corporate economist* implied that the job could indeed be done, and done well; in other words, the *need* for good planning was surely clear, so management might as well go ahead and label it as such and carry on! In the early postwar period, the fact was missed that it might not be possible to deliver what the position actually promised.

Just before the closed economy of the 1950s and 1960s broke down and the internationalization of the U.S. economy began, the technology of large mainframe computers arrived on the scene and promised economists a new lease on life. The application of statistical methods to economic data via large computer models, employing initially dozens and later hundreds and even thousands of simultaneous equations, was called econometrics. In the early days, only a few experts understood how to program computers for this task and outsiders were naturally awed by the accomplishment of the electronic task itself, quite apart from whether or not the results had any actual correlation to reality. No more powerful method of analyzing economic affairs had ever been applied, the observers thought, than these new computer runs—and it thus stood to reason that the results were as powerful as the method.

The debut of computer forecasting, or certainly one of the most important single instances, occurred in 1972 when research done at Massachusetts Institute of Technology (MIT) was published in *The Limits to Growth*.[4] This book provided the public with its first wide exposure to the techniques of computer modeling and the mere fact that the forecast had been done on computers seemed to lend inordinate credibility to the book's thesis. The public infatuation with *Limits* and its computerized analyses was immense. And at just about this same time, the rulers of Islam became acutely discontent with the price of oil at $1.80 per barrel and they attacked the western world with the OPEC (Organization of Petroleum Exporting Countries) oil embargo. The price of oil skyrocketed and *The Limits to Growth* seemed prophetic.

Also at the time of OPEC's initial price attack on the West, the Bretton Woods monetary agreement was abrogated. Not only did oil prices rise but so did the price of gold, other precious metals, commodities, and all raw materials. Exchange rates began a new era of volatility.

The demand for oil, even at quadrupled prices, continued to increase and many countries borrowed money to pay for it. The increased oil revenues went first to OPEC countries and then to their international banks, which recycled the funds back to the oil users. A global capital marked emerged, generally referred to as the Euromarkets. In the late 1970s, more Eurodollars were created than the total of all domestic U.S. dollars. This "off-shore" money was outside the control of the U.S. Federal Reserve Bank, but it was nonetheless real. It could be borrowed; it paid bills. By the mid-1980s, over $2 trillion in Euromoney had been created and annual interbank trading in Euromoney rose to $75 trillion. This is about 25 times greater than the funds needed for world trade of all goods. In addition, foreign exchange trading rose to about $35 trillion per year in the same period, about 12 times greater than actual physical trade.

Business Week called the new foreign exchange markets of the 1980s "casinos." Foreign exchange takes place in trader-to-trader speculation, in the same manner as commodities futures markets, although as yet mainly without designated pits and formal rules of the game. These exchange markets provide rational ways for participants to lay off risks in a very uncertain world. But such markets are notoriously unsuited to economic analysis based on the logic of supply-and-demand scenarios.

The markets are only "rational" because they permit "emotional" participants (speculators) to enter into the action. Thus, the newest, most global markets of our day, the financials, are dually rational and emotional—to an extent that few professional bankers and bank economists will ever admit. As we head into the greater and greater presence of global financial casinos, forecasting—especially that based on econometric models— becomes less and less reliable.

Business author Peter F. Drucker called this emergence of global capital markets a "symbol" economy, as opposed to the "real" economy. He said, "Economists assume that the 'real' economy and 'symbol' economy will come together again."[5] But how can we be sure this will ever happen?

In fact, the changes in money creation, trade financing, and international competitiveness now appear to be permanent rather than cyclical. We may never understand in detail what caused them, as the causes of economic change are rarely simple. And it may be a long time indeed before economic theorists accept that there have been truly fundamental changes, and it will be longer still before they adapt their theories to account for them. Above all, they will surely be most reluctant to accept that it is the world economy in control, rather than the nation-state on which so much of economic theory still focuses.

Drucker says, "Practitioners, whether in government or in business, cannot wait until there is a new theory. They have to act. And their actions will be more likely to succeed the more they are based on the new realities of a changed world economy."

I would add that their actions will also be more likely to succeed the more they are based on what works, rather than on what does not. History shows that econometric forecasts do not work; their recent performance, furthermore, suggests that they are getting worse rather than better.

SIX DIFFERENCES BETWEEN MODELS AND REALITY

If my own experience is a guide, there will still be readers who are having a difficult time breaking away from the cultural myth that economics should work, that economic forecasts should be accurate, and that someone, somewhere is able to predict the future. Let me list and briefly discuss a half-dozen flaws in conventional econometric forecasting that I uncovered during a number of years of trying to let big models do my forecasting for me.

The following discussion may strike some readers as excessively negative. It may sound as though I believe in nothing but sheer uncertainty and indeterminacy. But such is not the case. I believe strongly in the power of the human intellect—as opposed to the models of a computer, in and of themselves. I believe in human thought overall, not just the branch of mathetmatical thought. And I believe that executives can and do make better forecasts of the economy than economists, especially when the executives have freed their mind from erroneous myths and have taken full ownership of the process of making better forecasts than competitors.

One avenue of attack on myths, though by no means guaranteed, is a frontal assault—and that is what follows here. In other words, let me try to clear the forest before building my own proposed (superior) structure.

- *Difference 1: In economic models, facts are facts. In reality, facts are slippery. Everything depends on your point of view and the context.*

Most of us have had the real-life experience of witnessing an event as fact and then learning that other observers give quite a different account of the event, according to their point of view and the context of explanation.

A good example in the economic realm is the U.S. recession of 1991–1992. It is certainly a "fact," is it not? And yet, as our analysis in Chapter 3 showed, the governors of this country's central bank were not sure of its existence until several months into it. But no such uncertainty will be registered in the data. The statistical data on GNP, which will feed future computer models, will omit the uncertainty of the Fed. The tablets of economic statistics will appear clear and factual: (1) GNP growth in fourth quarter 1990 equals −1.6 percent, (2) GNP growth in first quarter 1991 equals −2.8 percent, and (3) therefore, with two successive quarters of negative growth, "a recession in U.S. GNP occurred in 1990–1991." Nothing about the Persian Gulf War, nothing about the Congressional Budget Agreement, and nothing about the so-called credit crunch will specifically appear in the data. Only the pure numbers "−1.6" and "−2.8" will be considered by econometric modelers.

- *Difference 2: In economic models, government indicators are discrete and solid. In reality, government indicators are based on sampling. They are aggregates or averages that require theories and judgment by their authors, and they are subject not only to revision but to redefinition to suit political goals.*

Which of the numbers for GNP growth in 1990–1991 should be used in a model to forecast the future: the "preliminary" ones (the ones that made the news and on which many bankers and business executives actually based contemporary decisions), or the "revised" or "final" figures that drew a puzzled yawn from all the actors except economists, who tried to give new interpretations of what we *thought* we knew had happened two months previously?

The indicator revision shown previously in Figure 3–3 may be sufficient, but allow me to go back to a headline that caught my eye in 1984. The *New York Times* contained a story in the business section called, "U.S. Revising GNP of 1977, Adds 3% Growth."[6] According to the story, the 1977 GNP was being changed from 5.5 percent to 8.5 percent. "Most of the additional $58.2 billion in economic activity, the Department of Commerce said, was accounted for by $47.6 billion of 'improved adjustments for misreporting on tax returns' of small proprietors, and by estimates for people who filed no tax returns." A Department of Commerce official commented, "Most misreporting clearly stems from the desire of the taxpayer to evade taxes."

Here we encounter two terrible realities for would-be modelers:

1. Society is not made up of citizens and businesses eagerly trying to cooperate with government data collection—in fact, just the opposite situation exists. Many if not most citizens are at all times assiduously *hiding* data. The so-called underground economy is enormous, in the tens or hundreds of billions of dollars (especially when drugs, prostitution, and organized crime are included).

2. Government is willing and able to change final data by significant amounts and will do so many years after the data were thought to be official history. (According to the *Economic Report of the President for 1991,* the GNP growth for 1977, the year mentioned in the *Times* story above, is now counted at 11.7 percent nominal, that is, not adjusted for

inflation, and 4.7 percent real. The 8.5 percent figure mentioned in the *Times* story has thus been rerevised.)

• *Difference 3: In economic models, data are available for every variable; events can be quantified; statistical discrepancies can be ignored. In reality, events defy quantification; important factors cannot be measured at all, let alone with precision; and the data from complex organizations, such as countries, do not all "add up."*

I have already mentioned the importance of unquantifiable factors in connection with the 1990–1991 recession—namely the Persian Gulf War, the Congressional Budget Agreement, and the credit crunch. Many other factors that weight on the national psyche, and thus on our economic productivity, could also be mentioned—including such purely qualitative events as the Supreme Court confirmation hearings of Judge Clarence Thomas. Will our sexual harassment norms ever again be the same and will our very workplace be different in the future? Do qualitative factors affect the economy? Yes, of course. Are they measurable? No, not to the extent required by modeling.

I have not yet called attention, however, to the existence of statistical discrepancies in the national income and product account tables, the magnitude of which will surely surprise the reader. Before we examine the national figures, however, consider your own household and reason with me as follows: During any given period, the amount of money you spend must be equal to (1) the amount you earned plus (2) the amount you borrowed. Whatever you spent but did not earn must have been borrowed. If, of course, during the period in question you spent less than you earned, then the amount that you borrowed would be negative, that is, you would have increased your savings. We would all naturally expect that this simple logic at the household level would apply to any other economic entity regardless of its size. Things should add up: You should be able to spend only and exactly the sum of what you take in plus what you borrow.

Consider now a country, such as the United States, that trades with other countries. During any given period, does it not make sense that the surplus (or deficit) of what we earn from trade should be equal to the change in what we borrowed or what we saved—which economists refer to as our capital account? In other words, if we sell foreign countries $25 billion more of goods and services than what we buy (which is referred to as a $25 billion surplus in our current account), should not that $25 billion show up in our bank account as an earned surplus (a savings)? On the other hand, if we sell less to foreign countries than what we buy from them, must we not also find a way to borrow the money to do this? However, examine the series of numbers on the facing page from the U.S. International Transactions Table, published by the Department of Commerce.[7]

The figures tell two stories: one in terms of their content and another in terms of their form. The first story is that, as a country, we have been selling far less to foreign countries than what we buy, and foreigners have been loaning us money by means of investments in our capital account (for example, treasury bills and bonds, properties). The second story is that the current account balance and the capital account balance *do not balance*—there is a discrepancy of many billions of dollars, money that is inferred to have flowed between commercial enterprises but that is not actually recorded in any government samplings. It is not possible to tell whether the trade figures are off, or the investment and banking figures, or both, or by how

Year	Current Account	Capital Account	Statistical Discrepancy
1980	$1.5	$−26.9	$−25.3
1981	8.2	−26.8	18.7
1982	−7.0	−27.4	34.4
1983	−44.3	35.1	9.2
1984	−104.2	80.3	23.9
1985	−112.7	97.4	15.3
1986	−133.2	121.9	11.3
1987	−143.7	141.8	1.9
1988	−126.5	137.2	−10.6
1989	−106.3	87.9	18.4
1990	−92.1	28.6	63.5

much. In the case of 1990, as the reader can plainly see, the statistical discrepancy is the largest for the entire decade.

Regardless of how nice it would be for modeling, precision measurements of global economic activity are not presently being made. Such measurements in fact are not even theoretically possible. If the United States itself is out of balance, what should modelers do, for instance, with the hundred or so less developed countries that have far less sophisticated national economic reporting systems than we do? And what should modelers do with the whole question of credit? In human affairs, does not credit seem to emerge as if it were our ultimate wildcard? What model, for instance, can assign a reliable limit to how much credit we can create?

- *Difference 4. In economic models, equilibrium is assumed to exist; from this base, events cycle. In reality, the universe is not obliged to be in any given condition, let alone in equilibrium.*

The previous example of statistical discrepancy takes us naturally to the next difference, which concerns equilibrium. Who would argue that human affairs are always smooth, well balanced, and under control? Who would dispute the importance of discontinuous events in history, such as wars, famines, embargoes, and unforeseen calamities like earthquakes and floods? Was the economy of Armenia a few years ago untouched by the death of tens of thousands in an earthquake? Was Bangladesh's GNP unaffected by the typhoon of 1991? Was Yugoslavia operating at equilibrium during the civil wars of that same year? How does one put equations around the demise of Soviet communism, or the sudden reversal of market orientation in China after the military intervention at Tiannanmen Square in 1989?

Over the very long term, human history shows a great degree of resilience, but over the shorter term, it can be seen that large societies and empires will decay, collapse, and vanish. If there is a rhythm to human affairs, as many experts believe, then I would say that it is complex beyond analysis. The science of mathematics itself, at least until very recently, has not been able to capture discontinuous events—such as when a twig under stress will finally snap, or when a population pushed to the brink will finally revolt. Mathematical formulas apply mainly to smoothly functioning mechanisms, like pendulums and spinning tops. The new science of chaos may help us out of this limitation, but as yet not enough is known to apply it to modeling.

- *Difference 5. In economic models, there are both dependent and independent variables. In reality, there are no independent variables.*

On June 5, 1985, the chief economist for Saloman Brothers of New York, Henry Kaufman (a man referred to in news stories as an "economic guru"), testified to Congress on the difficulty of defining *money*, especially as done by the Federal Reserve Board with its various official aggregates, M-1, M-2, M-3, L, and so on. He said that we should question "the validity of targeting some narrowly defined concept of money as a way of influencing the behavior of the economy," because "increased versatility of credit card usage, computer access by many to funds transfers, and virtually instant investment allocations" make *money* too hard to define.

No problem has been debated more often in economics than the definition of money. But the question remains open: Is it the supply of money that drives economic activity, or is it the strength of economic activity that drives the demand for more credit, and thus more money? Which is the dependent variable and which is the independent one? Is the supply of money more important than the rate at which people use it (that is, its velocity)? Which is the dependent variable: money supply or money velocity? Models cannot be constructed without answering dozens or hundreds of such questions. But in reality, forces act in the raw and in unforeseeable combinations—we are never sure how many are present, what their best names are, and which ones are most important.

- *Difference 6. In economic models, the economy exists as an aggregate entity. In reality, the economy doesn't actually exist. There are really just 250 million separate people, each with their own goals, falling into a myriad of different groupings.*

There is no such thing, in reality, as *the American economy.* The United States is made up of a network of competing economies, some of which sometimes prosper at the expense of others in the same network. These competing economies are connected, some more and some less, with other competing economies aboard. Even within a single competing economy in the U.S. network, there are apt to be competing interests.

For instance, in American agriculture a high price for corn is not desired by all farmers. A high price for corn is good for one type of farmer (the grain farmer), bad for another (the livestock farmer, who earns more when he can feed cheap grain), and irrelevant to others (the tobacco farmer, who is protected by tobacco legislation, or the vegetable farmer, who needs immigrant labor and is affected more by immigration laws). So a sector of *the economy,* such as agriculture, should also not be thought of as a single entity but as a group of sometimes competing interests, moving at different speeds according to different motives.

Special-interest groups have a bad name today, but there are really nothing but special interests. Each of us has our own special interest at heart. Congressional leaders understand this as well as anyone, despite their urging us to speak with a unified voice. Constituencies are not homogeneous. They can never really speak with one voice, but only with contradictory and competing motives.

ECONOMIC DATA ARE NOT
SELF-EXPLANATORY

The preceding discussion of differences between models and reality is merely a prelude to the main difficulty faced by

---

economic forecasters—all of us, whether or not we use large computer models, and whether or not we are professional economists or amateurs. The difficulty is so basic as to become the philosophical hub of everything I have to say in this book: Data are one thing; the *connections* between data are another. The data may be as accurate as you like, but the connections between the data are only as good as the mind that conceives them.

The professional economist reading these words will say, "He is challenging the scientific method. He is claiming that truth cannot be discerned by rigorous, empirical procedures."

My answer is that, in attempting to find better ways to forecast, I am indeed questioning the scientific method, but only in the sense of whether it actually *applies* to the realm of economics. I claim that "logical" connections between the data, such as one finds under scientific or mathematical examination, may have limited value to forecasters—because the human beings with whom we are concerned have dual motivations, partly rational, partly emotional. I further claim that the predisposition toward scientific method in processing the data has a way of removing the intellectual obligation to own and judge the arguments about what the data mean.

Consider my argument from the point of view of the well-known complaint that economists all talk in circles. Examples are abundant, but let's take the case of explaining the value of the U.S. dollar. In the mid-1980s, it was a surprise to most people to see the dollar rise strongly against foreign currencies, especially as the country was running a large trade deficit and federal budget deficit. As is always the case, there were several schools of thought on how this had come about. The two most dominant theories were as follows:

Theory A: Deficit Starts Everything

1. The federal government runs a fiscal deficit.
2. Therefore, government has to borrow more money than normal.
3. Therefore, borrowers are crowded out of the common pool of savings and credit (money supply), which is being kept tight by the Fed (which means low inflation).
4. Therefore, interest rates increase.
5. Therefore, the dollar is strong.
6. Therefore, a trade deficit develops.
7. Therefore, merchandise payments flow out of the country.
8. Therefore, foreigners have money to invest back in the United States to earn high interest rates.
9. Therefore, capital investment flows into our country from abroad, in essence serving to finance our government deficit.

Theory B: Capital Flows Come First

1. The United States is an attractive place for investment, due to high economic growth, high profits, low taxes, and high political stability.
2. Therefore, capital investment flows into our country.
3. Therefore, the dollar is strong.
4. Therefore, foreign goods are cheap.
5. Therefore, a trade deficit develops (if foreign goods are of sufficient quality to be desired).
6. Separately, heavy defense spending is required to keep our country safe and stable.
7. Therefore, a federal budget deficit exists, unless Congress cuts spending in other areas.

Both of these arguments are familiar and we have all heard the arguments in favor of and against them. Both of them make sense, but they differ in what can be called the direction of causality. In other words, each argument is a circle of logical elements. In Theory A you start at one point and travel in one direction. In Theory B you start at another point and travel in another direction. Many of the points of the arguments are the same—you just approach them up one street instead of another.

Theory A and Theory B about the dollar are examples of *economic circularity.* The person listening to the theories doesn't know which one is correct. A good speaker, whether economist or politician, can make either one sound right. An economist does this by saying that the data make it so; a politician does it by intonation and moral appeal. For many years now, listeners, who have gotten generally skeptical of politicians, have been taking economists at their word—that the data bear out the arguments. But this too is happening less often, as it dawns on listeners that the economists are no more right about the future than the politicians are.

Economic circularity is caused by the fact that data have no direction. Data are points. Connections between points must be made by those who use the data. Data do not, in and of themselves, demand to be connected in one and only one direction.

To believe that economists submit the data on the economy to the scientific method in the same way that chemists work out the formula for a new compound is a serious flaw in critical thinking, and one that will starkly limit the ability of an executive to win the amateur championship of forecasting. Chemists (and other professionals in the hard sciences) have two advantages over economists: (1) They can connect the data in any way they like and then test their theory against reality, over and over, and (2) if they have insufficient data to complete a theory, they can measure the compound anew, from as many different ways as they like. Economists can test theories only against other theories. History itself is, after all, only a theory, subject to vast differences in interpretation. Economists cannot go back to the lab and make more measurements; they are stuck, let's say in the case of U.S. GNP, with what the government publishes (first as a "prelim," then as a "revised," then as a "final," and then after a few months or years as another "re-revised").

The reader might at this point begin to wonder if this book is on its way to recommending the complete abandonment of data and of scientific method. Such a reader might ask, "You wouldn't say that we should close our eyes to the data, would you? Isn't it better to go as far as possible with scientific methods before backing off to a compromise position? Don't most economists compromise? They're not all *purists*, are they?"

It is true that many if not most economists compromise, but I would say that they are forced to against their will. The goal of the discipline is to push science, to the exclusion of all else, as far as it will possibly go—in the hope (and belief) that it will one day go all the way. My view is that this does not work and that a purely scientific approach to economic forecasting must be challenged before the reader can adopt more useful attitudes. The need for a more balanced approach must be recognized *before*, not after, science fails.

5

The Search for Gurus

Facing up to the fact that economics does not work and that forecasts are almost always wrong is not an enjoyable task; in fact, many will find it downright threatening. For those people, it will be more comfortable to stay put, secure in the belief that all questions have answers and that science can supply the answers if it is allowed sufficient time and sufficient means.

Virtually nothing can be said to dispel such a belief. It might be called a core property of our culture. It is the basis of a multibillion-dollar market for economists who say they have answers. The belief in the potential of finding "right" answers is so strong that this market grows every day, despite the fact that right answers are rarely if ever found and that no one is getting closer.

So it is a partnership of one person's fear of the unknowable and another person's optimism about being on the verge of scientific answers about human affairs that gives us economic gurus. The temptation to fill this role is something I personally have felt on many occasions. In fact, the catalyst for this book was an incident at my place of work that involved the temptation to become the "Answer Man."

A fellow worker, a scientist known for innovation in the company's research and development department, stopped me in the hall and said, "Bill, I need to talk to someone on your staff for five minutes to get some answers about the U.S. dollar."

I invited him into my office and picked up a copy of a one-page analysis that I had just finished preparing. In the wake of an announcement by the G-7 Finance Ministers that they were going to weaken the dollar by coordinated intervention, my one-pager gave the history of past Central Bank interventions and the lack of results against strong, underlying trends.

"Read this," I said. "It's hot off the press and tells you everything I know." My colleague (let's call him Jim) took the paper reluctantly, thanked me, and left.

In half an hour, Jim was back. Putting the paper down on my desk, he said, "This really didn't help. Let me explain what's going on. I've been working for the last two years on a pesticide formulation that works better than anything we've ever seen and I've got one of our best customers interested in giving it a test market—but now there's a hitch. One of the chemicals is only made in Europe and they sell it to us in foreign currency. That ingredient is a pretty big part of the cost, so I've got to know what the dollar's going to do before I can really recommend going ahead with the whole project."

A little nervously, but with complete honesty, I said, "I don't know what the dollar's going to do."

Jim looked at me blankly.

I continued: "It's not my job to know what the dollar's going to do."

Jim's brow knitted and his eyes wandered around my office in search perhaps of a nameplate that would reassure him that he was indeed talking to the company's director of economic research.

"My job is to provide you with whatever you need so that you can make up your mind yourself about what the dollar's going to do."

"I can't read a whole bunch of books on economics," Jim blustered. "I thought that was *your* job."

"You're the one who has to take the positions. I don't get paid to take those positions for you."

"I can't be responsible for the U.S. dollar," he said.

"Nobody can," I agreed. "But didn't you just tell me that you were responsible for estimating the cost of your new formula and isn't the dollar a part of that cost?"

He leaned forward and said. "Do you or don't you think the dollar will keep getting weaker? It may cancel my project, but just give me the bottom line and I'll stop pestering you."

"Look, it's not a case of my being too busy," I said. "I'll be glad to spend as much time as you want, pull together data you believe might help, test any positions you already have, or whatever—so that you can make up your mind."

"I can't *do* that!" Jim said. "I'm not the expert on economics— you are!"

Seeing that we were on different wavelengths, I offered another suggestion. "Why don't you ask that one of the company's commodities traders to be put on your development team? There are several who get paid to take positions on currency."

Jim shook his head, tossed up his arms, and started out of my office. "All I wanted was a simple answer to a simple question," he said.

In the silence of my office after Jim's departure, I contemplated the gulf between us. Jim was a professional scientist. He was expecting me, whom he regarded as another professional scientist, to share with him the fruits of my discipline. The first problem was that I did not regard economics as a scientific undertaking, and that in itself may have shocked him. But more likely, what it did was to complicate his life. After two years of effort on his improved formula, he would certainly be distressed by the impingement of some "extraneous" factor, such as the dollar, and he would be in the perfect mood to wish for some magic spell to make it go away. Perhaps he wanted me to perform the magic. Then I thought, "No intelligent man living today would believe, upon careful examination, that economics is a science—especially not another scientist. The evidence of failure, the lack of results from the scientific method, is too great." But Jim was not making a careful examination; instead he was simply following a longstanding custom. In the process he was willing to accord me, on the spot, some sort of extrarational or spiritual ability. That would solve his problem, at least in the short run. He could take my word on the path of the dollar and put the problem out of his mind. Later, if I were *wrong* and his project failed, he could point to my erroneous forecast and be absolved himself. And so, just now, he had gotten angry because his guru-designate would not play the game. On top of this, I had had the gall to suggest that predicting the basic uncertainty affecting his project was his own responsibility, not mine. How odd it must have seemed!

I then lapsed into sorrowful amusement in considering the corollary problem of how Jim's boss, and his boss's boss, could have permitted a project to go on for two years, a project that hinged so directly on the one economic variable that is the most uncertain and the least likely to forgive the frailties of economists, namely the future strength of the U.S. dollar. How many millions of dollars had the company spent on the project? And how many billions of dollars were being similarly put to risk in the whole United States, hostage not just to advancing the frontiers of chemistry (or some other legitimate science) but unwittingly to extrarational belief in gurus?

A strong demand exists for becoming an economic guru, to relieve others from facing the full uncertainty of the future. But the alternative, which is no more than plain honesty, offers a more powerful approach to improving business strategy. Forcing executives to take ownership of their own economic forecasts keeps them from trying things that are too risky and makes them prioritize avenues more realistically.

6

Business Without Economists?

The changes in approach I am recommending were conceived in the context of a rather large business with a chief executive and a corporate economist. The changes are still most easily explained in this big-company context, but their applicability is broad. If you are simultaneously your own chief executive and your own chief economist, then the following changes will be just as beneficial for you as for the functionaries I will be rhetorically addressing.

The changes I recommend are in one sense massive but in another sense small. For instance, I do not recommend that we entirely do away with all experts or with computers. Instead, I argue that if both we and our experts will change our philosophical outlook, we will together stand a much greater chance of beating the competition in this present age of uncertainty.

The idea that people should change their entire philosophy is, of course, overwhelming. But it may not be as hard as it sounds. The new philosophy that I propose is not totally unfamiliar. I have seen cases in which the switch has been made as soon as it was recognized that the option was available.

In other words, my new position is by no means unnatural; in fact, I would argue that the thing that is most unnatural is the belief that a business executive, in order to make the most profitable decisions, must be presented with the truth about economic conditions in his or her future markets—and that this truth can actually be obtained by scientific data processing of numerical indexes in computer models.

What the executive must do is to accept full and total responsibility for decisions and for the knowledge required to make them sound. What the chief researcher (whether an internal or external expert) must do is abandon the forecasting of truth (guruism) and adopt the role of adjutant to the executive whom he or she serves, closely supporting that person's pursuit of fuller knowledge.

THE NATURE OF REAL
BUSINESS KNOWLEDGE

The cornerstone of the failure of economists has been the mistaken view that knowledge does not exist in people, but only in books, data tables, and computers. Real knowledge exists only in real people. Businesspeople succeed according to whether they have better knowledge of situations than competitors. The knowledge they possess is contained in their own minds, nowhere else. They may have been helped in the formation of that knowledge by written reports, charts, memos, and so on, but it is only what they fully incorporate in their minds that makes up their living knowledge.

The principle that the human mind is primary (as opposed to such extrasomatic resources as books) has long been a part of formal philosophy. Perhaps the best view is given by the nineteenth-century philosopher John Henry Newman:

> Great as are the services of language in enabling us to extend the compass of our inferences, to test their validity, and to communicate with others, still the mind itself is more versatile and vigorous than any of its works. . . . It determines what science cannot determine, the limit of converging probabilities and the reasons sufficient for a proof. . . . Nor is it by any diagram that we are able to scrutinize, sort, and combine the many premises which must be first run together before we can answer duly a given question. It is to the living mind that we must look for the means of using correctly principles of whatever kind, facts or doctrines, experiences or testimonies, true or probable, and of discerning what conclusion from these is necessary, suitable or expedient.[1]

Today's executive knows very well that his or her decisions are as much affected by rumor, hearsay, and gossip as by detailed study of facts and logic. Newman understood this. In 1878, Newman listed "tradition, analogy, isolated monuments and records, ruins, vague reports, legends, the facts or sayings of later times, language, and proverbs"[2] as part of the array of methods that the mind must sort through in building genuine knowledge. But today's business executives feel compelled to hide from this. They seek to appear rational at all costs, to such an extreme that they deny their own humanity, along with their potential to enhance profits. They are often at conflict within themselves, trying to reconcile what they believe in their heart and soul and what someone is telling them they should believe on the basis of some or another economic model.

The economist, especially the econometrician, has in essence been telling the executive, "You're a dummy. You can't possibly know all there is to know. You certainly can't begin to know, in your head, all the economic factors I've got modeled in this 1,000-equation package."

Strictly speaking, the economist is right, but that is irrelevant. What the economist has in the package is not knowledge but chess. As we all know, the game of chess is ruthlessly logical, and it will thus be no surprise one day when computers beat the best living players. The province of computers is logic, not knowledge. Chess does not require knowledge, in the truest sense; it requires elaborate logic. Personnel departments are not instructed to recruit business candidates from chess clubs; if a top business executive happens to be a chess master, that is a coincidence.

THE ILLATIVE SENSE

I continue further with the eminence of the single human mind, and by way of an example introduce a term for the intellectual function of crucial importance to success in business. The example comes from comparing business with warfare (which is much more fruitful than comparing it with chess). Suppose Napoleon is on a hill, surveying the coming battle. He has toured his own troops and has them stationed where he wants them. He is now studying the terrain and the position of the enemy. After a few minutes, during which he has remained silent, he points to a wooded area down the hill on his right and says, "We'll attack through the woods at dawn." His lieutenants prepare to carry the order to the troops. They have just watched the great general apply a lifetime's worth of knowledge to a particular situation and they are willing to bet their lives that his knowledge is the best available.

The faculty that Napoleon exercised in this example is called the *illative sense,* which uses the entirety of our reasoning faculty. This is not the same as intuition, nor is it what is usually meant by "gut feeling." The illative sense involves genuine reasoning, taking into account not only logic and a lifetime of previous experience but new information, scouting reports, topography, and so on. Intuition and gut feelings are usually applied when one is operating without sufficient facts. The illative sense makes use not only of facts but also of the full array of evidence and of previous experience.

A crucial fact about the illative sense, from the standpoint of my own arguments, is that its operation will not usually be fully explicable by its owner. In other words, a good general may not be able to explain the details of why the march should proceed in a certain manner; he simply *knows* that it should. The belief, "If you can't explain it well, you must not know it well," is wrong. It is damaging misunderstanding of the illative sense. In fact, forcing a competent executive to explain himself to the nth degree will often interrupt the illative sense and destroy its soundness—especially if the executive subscribes to the fallacy that living knowledge can be fully explained to others.

Suppose one of Napoleon's lieutenants has scouted the woods. He says to the general, "Sir, I have been partway into the woods. There is a stream with no fords, so perhaps we should carry timbers with us." Or, "I have prepared a map of the woods, showing the pathways and streams." If the general and his lieutenant then join together in careful scrutiny of the map, it can happen that the general's illative sense will be enabled to make a more fully informed decision about the battle than before. This is the type of partnership that the executive and his or her chief researcher (or other experts) should seek.

But before elaborating on how to carry out this kind of partnership, let me summarize the reasons once again for seeking to undertake it. Changes in outlook are required both by the executive and by the chief researcher, which is the generic label I've chosen for the former position of corporate economist. Table 6–1 is addressed to the executive and Table 6–2 to the researcher; they summarize the philosophical changes necessary to a new partnership. The reader should study each of the figures before continuing.

The key to each figure is recognition of where, for business, the standard of truth lies. It lies in the market. Whatever the executive does should help earn more profits from the market and should provide greater longevity for the firm. Whatever the chief researcher does should further the executive's ability to earn money from the market. This may sound incredibly elementary, but it nonetheless requires all the emphasis possible.

Truth cannot be achieved in forecasting markets. What can be achieved is the ability to come a fraction closer to the truth than your competitors and to arrive there sooner. The function of forecasting and the ownership of any given forecast is the executive's, not the researcher's. The researcher can provide maps that may help the executive see how things work and may thus improve the potential of the illative sense to do a better job than the competitor's. But neither the executive nor the researcher should confuse the maps with reality; the reality that matters to profits is what the executive *knows*, in his or her mind, not what is in the computer.

The test of the new relationship between executive and

**Table 6–1   Changes in Outlook Required by Executives
Toward Experts—In Pursuit of Better Forecasts**

Abandon the view that:	*Adopt the view that:*
Truth is possible	Getting minutely closer to truth than the competition is possible.
Economics is a science.	Economics is a child of politics and culture. Human nature cannot be plumbed by science alone.
Economic gurus are responsible for forecasting truth.	Executives are responsible for forecasting. To win, they need teachers and systematic methods rather than faith—and the courage to examine their mistakes.
Econometric models will one day succeed, given powerful enough computers and large enough data bases.	Simple models, limited to two or three variables at a time, may help executives understand markets and do their job of forecasting better.
The economy can be known by mathematically integrating all its indicators.	*The economy* is a fiction. The economy is really millions of separate people and companies, with conflicting goals, enmeshed in government and culture, incapable of being precisely measured.

Table 6–2   Changes in Outlook Required by Experts Toward Executives—In Pursuit of Better Forecasts

Abandon the view that:	Adopt the view that:
Truth is possible	Getting minutely closer to truth than the competition is possible.
I am the guru. They should follow my forecasts.	My forecasts are usually wrong. Executives can and do make their own forecasts, and then they must live with them. How can I help them be rational while still supporting their inner, experiential grasp of their markets?
Forecasts should be made with many scenarios, so that all the eventualities are covered.	Executives already know the possibilities. They need concepts that will help them to see the most likely scenario before their competition sees it.
What matters is the position I take, and whether I am right.	I should take positions more to illustrate how my arguments work than to convince others to follow me.
Quantitative analysis underpins everything.	In our present age of uncertainty, qualitative analysis is usually more important than quantitative— often because competitors are not doing it well.
The substance is more important than its form.	Form and substance are equal. Presentation is 50 percent of the job. High-quality graphics and clear writing are crucial.

researcher is the market. The chief executive asks about the research, "Does it give me more confidence in configuring my assets?" and with time, "Are my assets more profitable than they were, considering my competition and considering prevailing conditions?" The marketing manager (or the trader or the sales manager or the finance manager) asks, "Does the research give me new concepts that allow me to adapt to daily realities in the marketplace faster and more accurately than my competition can adapt?"

7

Reclaiming Your Forecasts

The goal of this book is to foster a new attitude about what economics is (and is not) and what business should do with economics.

Experience shows that the forecasts of economists are notoriously wrong. But surprisingly, as business executives, we continue to sit through such forecasts without taking up arms in search of something better. The hope we all have for economics is automatic and eternal, despite its lack of results.

Upon reflection, of course, we all know that economics is not a science in the same way as chemistry or physics. The laws of economics are in no way comparable to the mechanical laws of motion. But because of the myth of economics as science, executives have fallen into the habit of making a qualitative separation between outlook and strategy and focusing almost entirely on the latter. Executives have given away ownership of their own outlook.

Whatever we mean by the *economy*, it is surely something that enmeshes and influences every customer and every company. If today we preach the goal of knowing our customer better, then how can this be done without simultaneously knowing the economy better?

In many cases, nothing I can say will change the determination of a firm to stay within the cultural norm—that is, to revere professional economists as though they were all Nobel scientists, whose theories *should* work (but do not).

Every executive, through his or her direct touch with the "pulse" of the market, has a headstart on professional economists in coming to a better overall economic outlook. Many executives, however, consider their own outlook of the economy to be amateur compared to economics professionals. This consideration would be a legitimate worry if the professionals were always (or even frequently) correct. But they are not. It is the amateur championship of economic outlooks—the one played between executives of competing firms—that really matters. The question is not whether all executives are amateur economists or not (they are) but what to do about it. Whether the CEO likes it or not, his job is to coach a team of amateurs and raise their level of play versus other such teams.

For the executive who changes his or her attitude, it is possible to see economics as a vast intellectual resource—like history, mathematics, or physics—that expands the more you know of it, but that does not require mastering every detail before becoming useful.

For one thing, economics is an inescapable ideal, an ideal at which to aim our behavior and also a framework of analysis that the human mind cannot ignore. Second, economics is an accepted tool of government policy. There is no larger, more serious user of economics than government. This in itself justifies a better understanding of economics by business executives, for two reasons: (1) to defend themselves against policies that may be seen to curtail business freedom, and (2) to better foresee the likely course of government action and its impact on industries, markets, and customers.

But economics is not an actual blueprint of human behavior. If I were forced to define economics rigorously, I might well focus on *The New Palgrave, A Dictionary of Economics* as a kind of physical index of the underlying reality. My definition might go something like this: "Economics is a complex body of thought about human behavior, the standard dictionary of which consists of thousands of articles written by hundreds of authors, no single one of whom can be said to understand every important principle in detail."

The most troublesome presumption we can all make as laypeople—which I have referred to earlier as the myth of economics as a science—is unthinkingly to believe that, yes, all of the entrees in *Palgrave* are necessarily, logically linked. This leads to a wholesale replacement of verbal principles with algebraic formulas, and then to an enormous intellectual error called econometrics.

The failure of large algebraic models of the economy (as used in econometrics) stems from the following differences between models and reality:

1. In reality, facts are slippery. Everything depends on your point of view and the context.
2. In reality, government indicators are based on sampling. They are aggregates or averages that require theories and

judgment by their authors, and they are subject not only to revision but to redefinition to suit political goals.

3. In reality, events defy quantification; important factors cannot be measured at all, let alone with precision; and the data from complex organizations, such as countries, does not all "add up."

4. In reality, the universe is not obliged to be in any given condition, let alone in equilibrium. The universe is the natural habitat of chaos and surprise.

5. In reality, there are no independent variables. Causal factors are interconnected and often act simultaneously.

6. In reality, *the economy* doesn't actually exist as a complete unit. Instead, there are 250 million separate people, each with their own goals, falling into a myriad of different groupings.

The habit of mind in American business is to assume that correct forecasts do indeed exist, at least somewhere—perhaps in large international agencies, such as the IMF, the Federal Reserve Board, or the large commercial banks and brokerages that employ famous economists. But examination of the track record shows just the opposite—the forecasts of prestigious organizations are almost always wrong.

The point for executives is, When do you expect to see the world's economic deck not have important wildcards, either financial, political, military, or other? Most will agree with me that the answer is "Never," Thus, it makes sense that you should consider recapturing the ownership of your economic outlook from the teams of experts whose methods make no adequate allowance for the unusual.

The business executive, in the interests of beating competition, must distinguish between the fact that (1) economics as a discipline has unquestionable value for business and government, but that (2) economic forecasting is virtually a complete failure.

In Part Two, I consider the question, "Who really needs economic forecasts?" and I then take the same approach to the discipline of business strategy as I did to economics: Is business strategy a science to be conquered with pure logic?

The answer, of course, will be that neither of the disciplines are sciences able to guide us toward perfection. But both disciplines, economics and business strategy, have parts that are useful, even powerful, for the executive who is willing to pick and choose, to experiment, and then to judge the quality of his or her tools by their results. The most power comes to an executive who determines not only to reclaim his or her own economic forecast but to strengthen the logical rigor of the strategy and to integrate the outlook with the strategy.

Part Three presents an array of creative approaches to making better forecasts.

PART TWO

Integrating Outlook and Strategy

8

Who Needs Forecasts?

In the past decade, there have been many articles confirming the propositions in this book, that economic forecasts are woefully inaccurate. For example, the headlines "Economists Are This Year's Endangered Species," "Economists Missing the Mark; More Tools, Bigger Errors," "Maybe Economists Should Be a Little Less Positive," "Economic Forecasts—We Need Them, But Can We Trust Them?" "Economic Forecasting: Few Hits, Many Errors," "The Prophets of Doom Have a Dismal Record," "The Science (Ha!) of Quality Statistics," "American Economics: 100 Years in a Rut," and "Oil Prices: Living with the Perils of Prophecy" all appeared in major newspapers and magazines in the 1980s.

There have also been many scholarly studies of the subject, for example, "Are Economic Forecasters Worth Listening To?" (*Harvard Business Review*, Sept.–Oct., 1984), "The Track Record of Macroeconomic Forecasts" (*New England Economic Review*, Nov.– Dec., 1983), and "The Accuracy of Individual and Group Forecasts from Business Outlook Surveys" (National Bureau of Standards, *Working Paper*, 1982).

If both the literature and the present author are correct, therefore, economic forecasts have for quite some time been more of a general blight on business than a boon. The question becomes, "How have we managed to conduct business at all, in view of how poorly we have forecast the future?"

HOW DO INVESTORS COPE WITHOUT GOOD FORECASTS?

The popular financial writer of the *Chicago Tribune*, Dan Dorfman, entitled one of his columns "With the Failure of the Pros, What's a Private Investor to Do?"[1] In this particular column, Mr. Dorfman summarized the results of a study that covered the performance of over a thousand "smart money managers," the ones who are paid big bucks for handling the money of smaller investors. The managers are the ones working for large Wall Street firms, who employ the majority of economists involved in forecasting. In 1984, these managers controlled over $300 billion of assets and their record for the year was abysmal:

- In mutual funds, only 12 percent of the pros beat the S&P (Standard & Poor's) index and 67 percent actually lost money.

- Among investment advisers, 19 percent beat the S&P and 53 percent lost money.
- In bank-managed, commingled funds, 20 percent beat the S&P and 44 percent lost money.
- In insurance equity funds, 22 percent beat the S&P and 39 percent lost money.

So one answer to the question of how investors cope is that they really don't—they continue to trust in experts despite heavy losses. This applies to large companies as well as individual investors. According to a study by *Petroleum Intelligence Weekly*, an aggregate investment on the order of half a trillion dollars was made by business around the world in 1980–1981 alone, "on the mistaken assumption that oil prices would rise steadily for the rest of this century.[2] Indeed, as I write this in the spring of 1992, the Third World debt associated with the oil boom and bust of the seventies and eighties remains over $1 trillion, leaving in its wake the near ruination of our entire banking system. And yet economists are still pursuing the same kind of econometric models on which the oil price forecasts were originally made and many executives are still buying the forecasts.

Although 1984 may have been a particularly bad year, Dorfman could have written nearly the same column every year since then, without really changing the title. As we frequently read today in the *Wall Street Journal*, the pros have a difficult time consistently beating a dart board.

But in all fairness to the experts, it may well be that we amateurs have unrealistic expectations about how solid we can ever make our investments. Perhaps in wishing for a level of surety that cannot realistically be attained, we in turn make unrealistic demands on the accuracy of forecasting. From a practical point of view, in other words, business always seems to cope with imperfect planning, if in no other way than simply to muddle through. To prosper, we must only muddle at a slightly faster rate than our competitors.

Furthermore, our drive for absolute certainty may be as much a function of linguistic platitude as anything else. A shrewd investment, we all learn growing up in a country like America, is one that yields a large return to our capital, does not involve a substantial risk of actually losing our capital, and is found by means of a keen financial acumen. The fact that we have the words for such an investment does not necessarily guarantee, however, that such an investment can actually be found, especially in the present day and age. The language about making a shrewd investment, though it has strong appeal, may simply be a survivor from our obsolete past.

Or indeed, the concept of a shrewd investment may always have been more of a platonic ideal than a prevalent reality. For instance, how do we know that in bygone days investors could be more certain of their choices than today? Picture yourself in the Middle Ages, at a coffee house in London (without a phone or a quote screen!), deciding to invest or not in a voyage to bring back gold from some new world, or deciding to underwrite the manufacture of a machine to gin cotton in competition with cheap slave labor, or deciding to buy bonds for a railroad to compete with other routes from Atlantic to Pacific across North America. How would you know which of these opportunities was low risk but high yielding any more than a particular stock today or a long or short position in Treasury futures?

Could it be that the words *investment* and *speculation* have always been much closer to synonymous than we would like to believe? In other words, could it be that a sound investment or a shrewd investment is one that can only be labeled with hindsight? At a given moment in time, we look up and see who is succeeding as a capitalist and we say, "That man is certainly a shrewd investor." True enough, perhaps, but only knowable after the fact. In this sense, capitalism is a system in which bets are placed on virtually every approach to making money but in which only a few of these avenues succeed, after which we rush to quiz the winners about how it was done. Often these proven experts do not really know how they did it and sometimes they cannot actually do it again.

Capitalism is also a system that has evolved in several long, overlapping stages, and it may be helpful to our perspective here to consider a simplified view of this historical process. The four main stages in the development of capitalism are as follows:

- Market capitalism
- Mercantile capitalism
- Industrial capitalism
- Financial capitalism

Each of these stages is built on and incorporates the earlier stages, but each of the earlier aspects of capitalism can still be found in full richness today. At the market stage, goods are brought to towns or fairs, offered at a price, bid for at another price, and either traded for other goods or sold for money. Credit, especially short-term credit, can also be a part of basic markets, but long-term credit comes into a whole new dimension during the mercantile stage, when trade voyages to distant lands are financed by letter of credit as well as by precious metals. The industrial stage sees the enormous investment of wealth in factories, technologies, and distribution methods—in the pursuit of greater profits by means of lower costs and higher manufacturing value added. It is probably this stage of industrial fixed investment that most needs a good forecast for its success. But in the absence of anyone's ability to foresee the future, capitalism has moved on. The final stage, financial capitalism, has to do with the hedging of capital requirements and the arbitrage of investment instruments.

In other words, the impossibility of predicting the future and the impossibility of being able to perfectly assess risk has led to the emergence, in Western capitalism, of such financial facilities as futures markets. These markets provide a convenient way to *bet* on what you believe will happen. For instance, if you believe that the price of a commodity will rise from its posted levels today, you may buy a contract to deliver such a commodity at some point in the future; if you are right, and the price does rise, then you will profit from your investment in this contract. If you are wrong about the future price level, however, you will lose.

Suppose, however, that you are against pure speculation but nonetheless need to use various commodities in your manufacturing business, commodities such as petroleum, whose price is known to be volatile and subject to great political uncertainty. In this case, you can buy the physical commodity, say at $20 per barrel, and simultaneously *sell* a contract for future delivery of the same amount of oil, which might also be at nearly $20 per barrel and timed to come due in six months when your manufactured product is ready for the market. In terms of the oil market, you are "hedged." You have one position in the physical market and another matching position in the paper market. If the price of oil in six months falls dramatically, let's say to $12, then you lose $8 from the physical side of your ledger, but you gain the same $8 back from the futures (paper) side of your ledger. (In other words, the futures contract that you sold for $20, six months ago, can now be fulfilled with $12 of oil.) By means of hedging, your manufacturing operation has thus been neutral to the price of oil.

The forecasting of price trends in and among futures markets, equity markets, and exchange markets is approached from three primary directions: (1) fundamentals, (2) technicals, and to a lesser degree (3) analytics.

The kind of economic forecasting we have so far been discussing is a form of fundamentals. The big problem with fundamentals—let's say the supply–demand–price situation in soybeans, crude oil, or copper—is that you can never know everything about all of the factors, you can never know how the relationship of the factors will change, and you can never know how other markets and political events will affect the commodity on which you are focusing.

The problem with technicals, which is the mathematical or graphical treatment of patterns of how action in the markets has behaved in the past (and which their adherents claim are models of the emotional side of investors en masse), is that the sudden emergence of a fundamental change (one usually not predicted by anyone, including the fundamentalists) will override the current technicals and launch a whole new pattern. In other word, technicals are fine unless the world changes fundamentally, which it always does.

Today there are futures and options markets for almost everything, or so it seems, either on recognized exchanges or by means of computerized synthesis. All of the major banks, brokerages, and computer companies have committed large resources to the development of software that will pinpoint (at lightning speed) tiny but lucrative differentials among the world's hundreds of futures, equity, and exchange markets—in a technological field called analytics. The goal of analytics is not actually forecasting but merely detecting opportunities for profitable arbitrage.

WHAT KIND OF PERSON REALLY NEEDS ECONOMIC FORECASTS?

A friend of mine who lives in New York comes as close to a modern day shrewd investor as anyone I know. My friend is an independent marketing consultant, involved with new approaches to reaching the public, with what the market wants, and with what works to get products sold. He invests in some of the companies he comes into contact with, if he believes that their product and their sales approach is "in tune with what works," and if he believes (on firsthand appraisal or by word of mouth) that the management team of the company is genuinely competent and/or well financed. The success of my friend's investment strategy does not depend on economic forecasting. Neither can his method be used by very many other investors, unless they are prepared to become independent marketing consultants.

And neither can the method be used by the companies themselves in which my friend chooses to invest. In other words, a given company cannot really choose to invest in another company with a better product, sales approach, and management team. A given company by definition is stuck with its own assets and liabilities. The company's executives want to know whether to expand and when, and into what kinds of new markets with the most growth potential.

As we discussed above, the most advanced form of capitalism—financial capitalism—is concerned with providing diverse opportunities to hedge against future uncertainties. It is also concerned with detecting and profiting from tiny differentials among hundreds of markets (sometimes with legitimate techniques, but sometimes too by bending or breaking the rules). As such, financial capitalism is not nearly so dependent on accurate economic forecasts as are companies involved mainly in what we have called industrial capitalism. The executives of these companies, responsible for making fixed investments of many millions of dollars for periods of five or sometimes ten or more years, are the main audience for the alternative forecasting methods developed in this book.

But let us be sure there is no other way. In other words, we began this chapter with the growing confirmation that economic forecasting has had very poor results, but that capitalism has coped by providing sophisticated tools for hedging in the face of uncertainties. Can a fixed investment, then, let's say in a large factory, be hedged?

With the advances in financial capitalism, it is indeed possible to hedge a substantial part of any industry's raw materials, and it is surely possible to hedge the interest rates and exchange rates on the capital required for a given business. But these hedges are for a relatively short period of time, usually for a couple of years. It is not really possible to hedge long-term investments in people, places, and facilities. There is not a futures contract for labor rates (though there is an inflation index contract), in particular let's say, for American rates versus European, Japanese, Chinese, or Russian. And although investing in a new factory in the United States is equivalent to "going long the dollar," in terms of how competitive the plant will be in world markets, there is no exchange rate futures contract long enough to protect the factory over a life of a decade or more.

It is also possible, without the use of any futures market, simply to design as much *flexibility* into long-term investments as possible—so that as economic conditions change, the capital asset can be altered, without starting again from scratch. But a "generic factory" that *gains* in flexibility will also *lose* in focus; in other words, at this point in the development of computer-controlled machinery, the general capacity still costs much more than the specific. Robots that can make "anything" are too expensive to be employed day after day on "something."

So ahead of making fixed investments, and afterward in terms of choosing the most profitable operating capacity or the size and timing of a marginal increase in capacity, business executives want to know what is going to happen with the economy.

Economist John Kenneth Galbraith, who agrees with me that forecasts are "inherently unreliable," offers a rather cynical view of why executives continue to buy econometric forecasts:

> The forecasts lift from the person who must make decisions as to the future a heavy, even perilous responsibility. Since he cannot know the demand for the fertilizer, urban office space, recreation vehicles or rail, air or road transport for which provision must be made, the forecast allows him to yield his judgment to the forecaster. If the judgment is wrong, it is not his; instead it is the best professionally available—a significant protection in a world of tense bureaucratic conflict.[3]

To paraphrase Galbraith we might say, "That which is essentially speculatory we prefer to call an *investment.*" And when it comes to decisions about large business investments, just as I observed earlier about planners, "Executives pretend they know what they're doing and investors pretend to believe them."

9

Strategy Without Economics

On purely the basis of word count, it would take no more than five years' issues of the *Harvard Business Review* to equal the 4-million-word total in *The New Palgrave, A Dictionary of Economics*. I think that each of these publications is a kind of representative index to its respective disciplines, business and economics, and that the comparison can help illuminate the myths we hold about each.

Let us briefly consider the academic discipline of business in the same fashion as we treated economics in Part One. Is business strategy a perfect science? Do professors of business think it could be or should be?

In any bimonthly issue of the *HBR* a current case study is featured, followed by four or five "solutions" offered by leading executives in the industry under question—and most often taking four or five entirely different approaches. Yet the business reader does not criticize *HBR* for providing contradictory principles. The business reader, I think, would scoff if only a single "Harvard-approved solution" were printed each month. "Every business situation is fabulously complex," such a reader might say, "and every situation can be approached in dozens of powerful ways."

The business reader, furthermore, does not stand back from the material in *HBR* (often quite formidable, with specialized terminology and sometimes formal mathematics) and say, "I have no use for all these theories." Instead, the business reader is apt to think, "I wish I had the time to digest all of this material and study it carefully. I know it would give me a few really good ideas and help me beat the competition."

At the Harvard Business School itself, extraordinary emphasis is placed on the case study method, which relies on putting the student mentally into the position of an executive surrounded by strategic threats and opportunities. The student is forced to make decisions aloud in class discussion and to support them rationally, after which his or her choices are subjected to aggressive critique by peers and professors. The experience is more lively, to say the least, than quietly working on number problems in one's dormitory. Students at the school eagerly attack dozens if not hundreds of these cases during a year's study; older participants in industry seminars are surprised by how many such cases they are expected to cover in, say, a three-day period.

Standing in front of the Baker Library of Business at Harvard, one does not imagine that the tens of thousands of cases, books, and articles inside should form a coherent whole, as one might think in front of an equally large collection of works on economics. In other words, one does not conceive that a computer model should be constructed from the thousands of business cases, a model in which all the principles are linked by means of hundreds of interlocking equations—so that the optimum strategy of any business could be determined at the push of a button, merely by plugging in a few coefficients. We do not customarily think of the body of business knowledge in the same way as we do economics, that it ought to be systematic (if not actually mechanistic). In business, we may accede that there are principles, yes, but they are often quite singular, always very messy, and in total nearly innumerable.

As if to contradict me immediately, however, sit two particular volumes on the shelves of Baker Library: *Competitive Strategy* (1980)[1] and *Competitive Advantage* (1985),[2] both by Harvard Professor Michael E. Porter. It might be said that Porter is to business strategy what the Chicago School is to economics.* Porter's is an effective, persistent voice proclaiming the power of *micro-logic,* an insistence on the potential of assembling powerful business systems from tiny parts in well-executed, algebraic steps, and of making that which is implicit in any rationale explicit. An executive standing in front of Porter's volumes may well have the same feeling as an economist in front of *Palgrave:* "If I can conquer this, I'll become a master expert.

Chapter 13 of Porter's second book, *Competitive Advantage,* is called "Industry Scenarios and Competitive Strategy Under

---

*One member of the so-called Chicago School of Economics, George J. Stigler, was quoted earlier in Chapter 2. "Of all the social sciences, only economists possess a theoretical system to explain social behavior." Another famous member of the group is Milton Friedman. The group maintains that rigorously applying the scientific method to the data of society will yield the most instructive results.

Uncertainty." This chapter contains Porter's main ideas about how business should deal with the future, which of course is always the main source of uncertainty. He says:

> Most strategic plans are based on single-point estimates about the future, usually the best guess of the managers involved. Rarely are managers able to perceive fundamental shifts in their competitive environment ahead of time, and find imaginative ways of dealing with them. (page 480)

Instead of trying hard to predict the future, Porter recommends the careful and complete development of special tools he calls "industry scenarios." These are based on his division of industry structure into five main elements: the power of buyers, the power of suppliers, the threat of new technology, the threat of new entrants to the industry, and the strength and kind of rivalry between competitors. In Porter's view, industry structure determines profitability, rather than mainly some underlying set of economic conditions. A particular firm can enhance its own profitability by means of strategic choices that are inherently constrained by industry structure: The firm can move between seeking a cost advantage in one direction, or seeking a highly differentiated product in the other direction. A firm can also try to narrow either of these generic strategies within a certain geography or a certain segment of the market (for example, targeting a certain age group, income class, and so on). But the firm is not free to create strategy out of thin air. In Porter's view, the main kinds of generic strategies are seen as preexistent, as if flowing from the very nature of capitalism and markets. As he prescribes his long list of systematic procedures for developing industry scenarios, Porter says:

> Constructing scenarios is a process of abstracting those elements of uncertainty that will drive strategic choices. Selecting and

analyzing a few scenarios from the range of future industry structures requires picking the most important cases and simplifying them. (page 470)

Industry scenarios, Porter claims, are not intended as forecasts. The emphasis is on implementing a kind of "military" process that will effectively replace the need to forecast the future, or at least the need to forecast it very accurately. The industry scenario process will allow the firm to "mitigate uncertainty or make a bet on the future mindful of the risk involved." The use of explicit industry scenarios "brings the uncertainty of planning out into the open," Porter says, and "bases strategy on a conscious and complete understanding of the likely significance of uncertainty for competition."

What does Porter mean here by the *complete* understanding of uncertainty for competition? Is he not substituting one impossibility for another?

One wonders how serious Porter really is about the full substitution of this scenario process for pure forecasting of the future. He tips his hand, I think, at one point in Chapter 13, when he admits that, "Early information about the future state of scenario variables has a high strategic value." To this mouthful of an understatement, I say, "You bet!'" Predicting the future right could have real value indeed.

And in reality, what executive could ever *not* have his or her implicit forecast? Can such a natural intellectual process as prognostication be completely repressed as if it were a bad habit—and then replaced by an essentially external process (such as Porter's industry scenario construction) on the grounds of its pure logic?

The purpose in reciting this extended example of business method, along with its own complexities and uncertainties, is twofold. I want to focus attention on the extremes in both disciplines: economics and business. In the same way a science of economics implies a human society in the form of a giant Swiss watch, the full application of Porter-style algebra to business strategy implies the existence of companies run by robots. For the Porter method to work in full requires managers who are perfect logicians.

And second, I want to call special attention to the considerable intellectual resources that executives can bring to bear on a subject when they want. Executives, when they see the potential for gaining competitive advantage, are fully capable of searching out, comprehending, and applying a complex intellectual discipline. When it comes to strategic thought, in fact, executives know that they must be up to their elbows in this pursuit, or they risk losing advantage by holding still. What I seek to argue in this book is the need for executives to roll up their sleeves and take back ownership of their own economic outlooks, which are just as crucial to success as their business strategies, but which have been turned over in error to professional economists.

The way to do this is to adopt a more humble posture than that suggested by either the Nobel laureates in economics or the Harvard professors of business. Neither of the disciplines are sciences, able to guide us toward perfection. But both disciplines have parts that are useful, even powerful, for the executive who is willing freely to pick and choose, to experiment, and then to judge the quality of his or her tools by their results. The most appropriate motto here is, "Take the best and leave the rest"—and it should be applied both aggressively and guiltlessly.

10

Real-World Strategy

Part One shows that many economists, and in particular many mathematical economists (econometricians), believe that a large, coherent set of rational laws govern human behavior, including the behavior of large groups such as companies, countries, and ultimately the entire world. The rules are waiting to be fully discovered in statistical data and then modeled with computers.

Part Two shows that some professors of business strategy, including at least one well-known professor-consultant at Harvard, believe that a set of rational rules can be found to describe the competitive interaction of firms without any further reference to the discipline of economics.

Which one of these two extremes is most accurate? Or perhaps more productively, where in between these two extremes should the executive look for the most powerful approaches to beating competition and increasing profits?

Is the economy best seen as an external environment of large fiscal and monetary forces that impinge on a single business, or is the economy merely the net result of all the competitive interactions taking place between millions of different, separate business? Suppose we take the view that the economy is nothing beyond the result of competitive interaction. Then, following the argument of Michael Porter, a single company can be described as a link in a "value chain" between suppliers and buyers, as shown in Figure 10–1. The function of the company is to begin with some form of raw (or intermediate) materials and to add enough value that a buyer will pay more than the company's costs for producing the finished product or service.

A single industry, in this view, is thought of as a competitive rivalry between two or more firms, fighting each other for suppliers on the one hand and customers (buyers) on the other, as shown in Figure 10–2. The degree of competitive rivalry characterizes the industry in question—the more highly profitable the firms are, the more attractive the industry is for new entrants (for new capital from shrewd investors), and the more likely it becomes that substitute products and services will be introduced (perhaps from outside the industry, through technological innovation).

After sufficient time, an industry can be characterized as shown in Figure 10–3, with intensive competitive rivalry. The degree of this rivalry, however, does not necessarily mean that all the firms will be low-profit—for some may adopt more powerful strategies than others, thus growing in size and margin. It is this feature of industry structure, the fact that companies all have a reasonable possibility of prospering at their competitors' expense—*regardless of prevailing economic conditions*—that makes the study of business strategy so absolutely compelling.

A flip side of this principle about competitive strategy is also true: Not even the best of prevailing economic conditions, accurately forecasted or not, can fully assure the profitability of a company if it is following an unwise strategy within its own

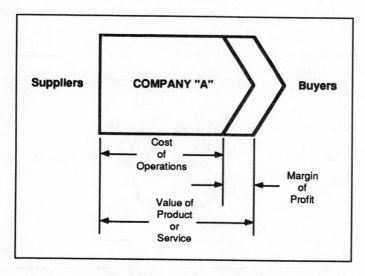

Figure 10-1. Single company as value chain between suppliers and buyers.

The basic function of a company can be seen as adding value along a chain between raw material supplies and the final buyer of a product or service. The company's goal is to add a much greater value than its costs.

(Source: Adapted from Michael E. Porter, Competitive Advantage, New York: The Free Press, 1985, p. 37.)

industry. Good strategy, in other words, is a sine qua non of good profits and of the long-term survivability of the firm.

But good strategy, by which we mean the positioning of a firm within the industry in terms of the relative costs and differentiability of its products and services compared with competitors, is not the only condition of success. If this were true, we could view the economy as a simple sum of the competitive action of all the companies presently in operation.

Where in such a fabric would we put such factors as a doubling of the price of oil (as happened in a few weeks during the Persian Gulf War of 1990), the collapse of communism (and

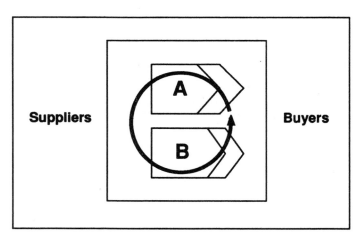

Figure 10-2. Single industry as a competitive rivalry between companies.

An industry can be seen as two or more companies competing for suppliers and for the sale of products or services to buyers. An industry such as in this figure, with few competitors and high margins, draws new entrants and substitute products and services, leading to greater competitive rivalry, as shown in Figure 10-3.

with it the imminent decline of U.S. defense industries), or the passage of the 1990 Clean Air Act (or any of dozens of other new environmental regulations)—let alone the decline of short-term interest rates in 1991–1992 to levels not seen in twenty years?

Clearly, it seems to me, the executive must see his or her company and industry as shown in Figure 10–4, embedded in some set of forces larger than just those produced by competitive action. A still more powerful view is shown in Figure 10–5, where the forces are not merely economic but also governmental, cultural, and international. A good forecast will have to

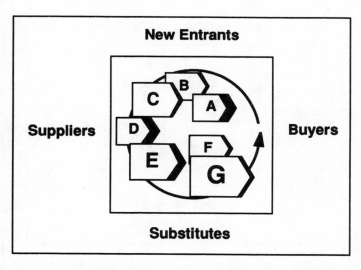

Figure 10-3. Single industry with intensive rivalry between many companies.

Within an industry, companies adopt different strategies to compete, and thus to grow in volume and profit. The choice of strategy usually depends more on competitive dynamics than on economic outlook.

do not merely with interest rates and capacity utilization but with politics, culture, and international affairs.

To earn substantial profits in business and to ensure a firm's survival over time has become increasingly difficult in the late twentieth century. The executive has little choice but to become smarter than the competition. The avenue recommended in this book is a path not covered either in prestigious

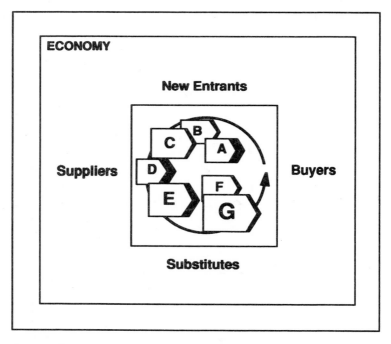

Figure 10-4. Companies (and their industry) embedded in economy.

A better approach is to focus on both strategy and outlook—to see the company and its industry embedded in larger economic forces.

schools of business or departments of economics. But in the face of slow or negative economic growth, in the face of a continual stream of international surprises, and in view of the mergence of new governmental regulations meant to meet the public's environmental agenda, it is time to take up whatever method works the best.

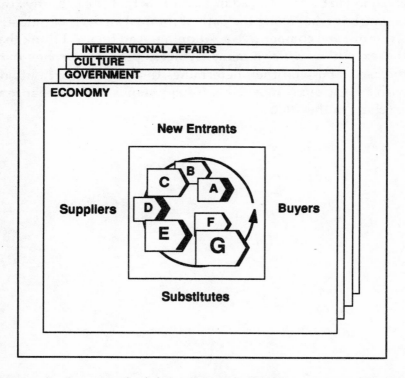

Figure 10-5. Companies (and their industry) embedded in economy, politics, and other forces.

An even more powerful approach is to see the company embedded not just in economic forces but also in government, culture, international forces, and various other layers.

What I urge is a new approach to both economic forecasting and business strategy. I think the executive can use his or her own pulse of the economy and make better forecasts than either the professionals or the other amateurs in his or her industry. The key is mainly attitude, along with a set of straightforward, consistent methods (some suggestions are given in Part Three). In addition, I think that the executive can go much further along the path of rational analysis of industry structure and competitive positioning. And finally, I think that the executive who reclaims ownership of his or her own forecasts and who then determines to integrate that outlook with a conscious competitive strategy stands the best chance at excelling in the 1990s.

PART THREE

*Making Better
Forecasts*

11

Accuracy in a World of Uncertainty

In a medium-size American company today, let's say with sales in the hundreds of millions of dollars, many tens of millions of dollars will likely be employed in inventories to cope with the pattern of consumer demand (for instance, if Christmas or some other season is the peak of sales) and to avoid having too much capital invested in overall factory capacity. The more accurate the prediction of how much inventory to carry, the less expensive it will be to do so, both in terms of warehouse space and of borrowed capital with which to finance it. An inventory in excess of needs by, say, $10 million over a year's time amounts to a loss of between half a million and a million dollars, depending on interest rates. An insufficient inventory, however, let's say again by $10 million, may mean the outright loss of business in this same amount, or more, including the profits associated with that business.

With so many millions at stake in the prediction of inventories, is it any wonder that top management puts pressure on the company's sales and marketing staffs, and on its economists, for accurate predictions? Sometimes, or so it seems to the staffs, the demand is for absolute accuracy, that is zero tolerance.

Inventory levels are only one aspect of how an accurate forecast can save money. Top management looks at how many millions are at stake and says, "Hire the best economists that money can buy and get the forecasts accurate. There are millions of dollars to be saved!"

And when the staffs and the best outside experts fail to hit the mark, as they almost always do, the reaction of management can often be, "Let's replace these guys with people are care about saving the company's money. Let's get people who will pay enough attention to forecasting to get it right!" This is of course an extreme kind of attitude, but in my experience it is by no means rare. When top management refuses to accept the responsibility for the inherent uncertainty of the firm's operation, the staff too is much more likely to pass the blame on to outside experts than to try to find new and better approaches to forecasting themselves. The reader who has come this far will be well beyond the kind of "stonewalling" I have just described and will be seeking more advanced ways to deal with the inherent uncertainties of forecasting.

The first two parts of this book have been aimed at combating the idea that economics and business can be treated as scientific disciplines. The goal has been to move the reader away from the misconception that economic forecasting and business strategy can be effectively treated mainly with numbers, mechanistic logic, and computer programs. In place of seeking the advice of world experts and the benefit of scientific approaches, I have suggested instead that the executive must compete in an amateur championship among his or her peers. In my view, forecasting is simply another aspect of business in which the goal is to beat competition—and in which the most effective tools are not preordained, including the Ph.D. in economics. Whatever works, works.

The third part of this book consists of an eclectic catalog of alternative approaches to making better economic forecasts. This chapter calls attention once again to the absoluteness of uncertainty and comments on the ranges of probabilities associated with business-level forecasting (regardless of whether the forecasts are made by "expert" economists or "simple" businesspeople). Chapter 12 emphasizes the one overarching method that unfailingly leads to better forecasts—namely, the honest comparison of forecasts with actuals, followed by ruthlessly throwing out what does not work and keeping what does. Subsequent chapters list and discuss some of the many techniques I have found that do work.

UNCERTAINTY IS ABSOLUTE

I have been speaking of science as if even in its proper domain it were a discipline that follows logic like an unrelenting robot. This is of course a vast exaggeration. In reality, science and uncertainty are tightly linked.

An alternative approach for this book, which at this point will surely seem ironic, would have been to inquire exhaustively into the intrinsic nature of science—for as we all know, the closer we come to the frontier of science, the less we need to remind ourselves of the presence of uncertainty. At any scientific frontier, uncertainty abounds, as if an automatic property of the universe itself.

The most celebrated formulation of the role uncertainty plays in science is surely the Heisenberg uncertainty principle first advanced in the 1920s and widely popularized since then. What Heisenberg discovered at the atomic level was a trade-off rule, similar to many such rules at the everyday level. Consider, for instance, the following situation in riflery. To hit a bull's-eye consistently, a marksman must fire from a fixed position. But as we also know from common sense, the more at rest such a marksman is, the better target he or she makes for an enemy marksman. A rifleman running at full speed makes the hardest target, but the trade-off in so doing is that he has the least ability to shoot straight himself.

At the atomic level, where particles can be detected only through their actions and reactions with other particles, Heisenberg asserted that an observer can never simultaneously measure both a particle's exact speed and its exact position. The universe has this trade-off built in. The principle holds regardless of the precision of our tools; in fact, the principle is a theoretic limit on the precision of any tool we can ever imagine. The more microscopically we probe to find a particle's position, say perhaps with a single photon of light, the more we simultaneously change the particle's velocity—because the measurement photon itself imparts added energy to the particle. We cannot really observe an aspect of physical reality without touching it, and in so doing we move or change the thing that we only wanted to measure.

Complete accuracy, therefore, is an unachievable intellectual ideal. In reality, knowledge of the world can only be approximate: We may attain a high probability of knowing where something is, and simultaneously its speed, but we never reach a 100 percent probability.

In digressing this far into the realm of physics, my hope is that by reminding ourselves of the fact that uncertainty is fundamental at the atomic level, it may be easier to acknowledge that uncertainty is likewise fundamental at the level of human life and society.

UNCERTAINTY MEANS TRADE-OFFS

Examples of trade-off rules abound in economics and business. Earlier in the book, I mentioned, for example, the problem of the government's having to revise and re-revise economic indicators. The monthly production level of a particular industry, for example, can only be sampled—and the sample that comes in on the bureaucrat's due date is usually incomplete. (Business complains loudly about having to comply with the government's reporting requirements in the first place and gives the questionnaire from the Department of Commerce a low priority.) But to wait for the complete sample, and thus perhaps for an indicator that is more accurate, may mean that the indicator has little value when finally published. It may be more accurate, but it will also surely be old news.

All market research in business faces the same problem. Executives would prefer to have complete information before making a decision, say to launch a new product. But to wait for the research to be performed may be to miss the best competitive window for rolling out the product.

Worse yet, complete information is not something that can actually be supplied to the executive at all, regardless of how long he or she is prepared to wait. There is a trade-off between

(1) acting immediately with little knowledge and getting market feedback, good or bad, and (2) studying the situation carefully before acting, but hopefully acting more wisely and reducing the chances of a bad response.

The emotional discomfort that any executive feels in making an important decision stems in great measure from the above trade-off, which is an inherent feature of competition. Early in life we are taught to look before we leap and to not make snap judgments, but we find with experience that the opposite extreme, which we may proudly call the fullest analysis of all the facts, will not unfailingly guarantee better results. The analysis may well require more time than we can spare to beat the competition to the punch. The analysis may also require more money than we can afford, and the conclusion of the analysis, regardless of time or money, may be just as indeterminate as our first impression. So the executive, compared with other kinds of professionals, may feel perpetually off-balance, wanting more information and better understanding before an important move but recognizing the trade-off in terms of time, money, and the odds of only a marginal improvement in certainty.

HOW GOOD CAN FORECASTS BECOME?

Let us move now from the absoluteness of uncertainty to the ranges of probability associated with business-level forecasting. Heisenberg's theoretical point about indeterminacy may be well taken, but at a practical level it is essential to learn to live with uncertainty.

Chapter 3 presents the record of the IMF, the Fed, and the Consensus of Economic Experts in forecasting a large aggregate, such as world or U.S. GNP. The record shows that, with a forecasting horizon of one year out, all the prestigious authorities will miss GNP by about 10 percent of the forecast range, and that frequently they will miss it by much more. Inevitably, every few years, they will even sometimes miss a big change in direction, by as much as 30 to 40 percent. To tighten these forecasts down to a horizon of a quarter or a month, and to focus simultaneously on a smaller aggregate (such as housing, metal fabrication, or mining), *increases* the range of forecasting error.

In economic forecasting, therefore, the trade-offs as Heisenberg might have expressed them are as follows:

1. The further into the future we wish to forecast, the less accurate we will be; but the closer to the event we are, the less value an accurate forecast will have.
2. The smaller the economic aggregate we wish to forecast, the less accurate we will be as well; but the more general, vast, and "macro" the aggregate, the less value its accurate prediction has to any particular business.

As previously mentioned, the commercial activities of an individual company take place within the broad context of a national and international economy, whose fluctuations are difficult indeed to predict. But the company itself can have a more accurate record of its own narrow activities than is possible for the economy at large, and the company will also (by the shear fact of being in business) take corrective actions to return to a predicted level if it falls behind—and this leads to the fact that a forecast for a single company need not be inherently less accurate than for an entire economy or some major sector.

THE HUDSON UNCERTAINTY PRINCIPLE*

Depending on the size and coherency of its business units or divisions, a company's annual forecasts of sales and profits may be more accurate than the results given above for authorities predicting world or U.S. GNP. In other words, a well-organized company should expert to make annual forecasts slightly better than the plus or minus 10 percent error mentioned above for projections of the entire economy, and it should expect to have fewer and smaller of the occasional large errors that occur when the fundamentals of the market change dramatically.

In terms of a quarterly or monthly forecast of sales, the following ranges and characterizations are possible:

5%	Impossible to maintain every month.
10%	Possible most of the time and credible with most managements.
15%	A general norm or average, but some managements may consider it "too sloppy."
20%	Bound to happen at least once or twice a year.
25%	Bad show. Forecaster did not see a wild card in time.

The percentages are stated as mean average percent errors (MAPEs) without reference to plus or minus.

---

*In preparing myself for a consulting assignment on improving the forecasting accuracy of a major U.S. manufacturer, I once examined ten years of articles in the *Journal of Forecasting*, plus all the other reported cases of forecasting accuracy I could find in the business literature. The Hudson uncertainty principle is based on a combination of this literature review along with my own personal experience in making forecasts and consulting forecasters.

Many exceptions to the above general rule can be found. The ranges grow much larger if the goal is to forecast not a general category of products or services but a specific size, shape, color, or price range. In other words, a forecast accuracy trade-off sets in which the product definition target is narrowed.

I have found, however, that top management will often be pleased to know about the existence of the above ranges and will begin to work with the forecasting staff to develop a specific set of tolerances that seems reasonable and consistently achievable for the company and its products or services.

12

Independent Thought and Honest Feedback

In the same way that investors search tirelessly for a flawless adviser, researchers of all kinds attempt to find magic methods that will lead them unfailingly (if not mechanically) to *truth*. But alas, the quest for patented formulas in forecasting is a failure.

Paradoxically, however, one cannot approach forecasting successfully without a method, and yet every method that has ever been tried becomes a trap, sooner or later preventing its user from perceiving a new trend or a wild card before the competition sees it.

Economists are trapped by their dedication to indicators, laws, and mathematical models. Historians are trapped by the shear wealth of historical detail and the need to mold the evidence into an entertaining story. Harvard professors of business are trapped by the plethora of case studies and a lack of coherent theory, or by the use of a theory that attempts to generalize the cases within the world of business itself without reference to the economic, political, and cultural forces in which business is enmeshed. Professors of all kinds, whether in the sciences or the humanities, are trapped by tenure and the syndrome called "publish or perish," and by journals insisting that every new idea be scientifically demonstrated (according to a jury of like-minded peers) before its dissemination.

Famous futurists sometimes originate entirely new and striking methods, but these too usually become traps. For instance, John Naisbitt, author of *Megatrends*,[1] says in his book that he relied heavily on the use of *bellwethers*—a term originally referring to a ram with a bell around its neck at the head of a herd of sheep. But just as we can conceive of a herd without such a ram, or a bellwether with no herd in tow, we can see that not every large trend can be spotted ahead of time by some faint signal in the hinterland.

My solution to the choice of forecasting method is simple, but not easy, especially for these executives hoping to discover some form of automation. I recommend independent thought and honest feedback. This combination requires trying things until you find what works and then carefully critiquing yourself after every forecast to pinpoint what went wrong, to learn something for the next round.

As trite as this answer sounds, however, my experience shows that the combination of independent thought and honest feedback is very rarely applied by businesses today, particularly honest feedback. Therefore, the method actually constitutes a surprisingly strong competitive advantage.

Suppose the forecasting process and its components are thought of as shown in Figure 12–1. The inputs to the forecast

---

are divided into two groups: those that are present every day, week, or month (which I label *normal* factors), and those occurring irregularly (which I label *singular* factors). For instance, the normal factors would include such inputs to the forecast as current sales, the pulse of business and the economy, and

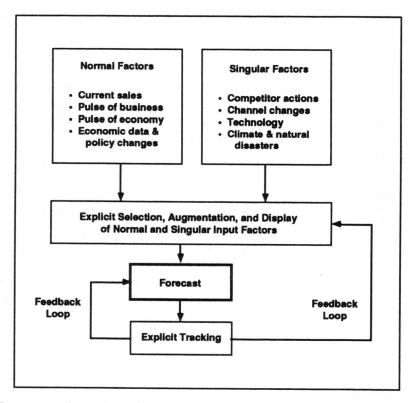

Figure 12-1. Forecasting components and process.

Better forecasting results mainly from greater attention to careful tracking of results, followed by modification of the methods used.

various (selected) economic data and policy changes. The singular factors would include such inputs as competitor actions and reactions, changes in the channels of distribution, new technology, and major events in weather or natural disasters.

These factors must be subjected to explicit selection, augmentation, and display. In other words, the forecaster or forecasting team must apply intelligence and judgment in deciding what to pay attention to, what to amplify, and what to put in the center of the main screen. A team must discuss this step openly and thoroughly. Then the forecaster or team must integrate all the factors into a single forecast. (Don't ask me for a step-by-step blueprint of how the mind works—it simply works.)

The main key is tracking the results and forcing the mind to see and accept its errors—after which it will find a better way to select, augment, display, and integrate the next time. Honest feedback is such hard work that few competitors will be willing to do it. Reviewing errors is terribly threatening to the relative positions of the people on the forecasting team. A boss is not supposed to be a person who makes mistakes. Most businesses prefer to forget the failures of yesterday or last week and start fresh.

Figure 12–2 elaborates on the structure described above, particularly in the treatment of normal factors. As shown, there is nothing wrong with subjecting current sales numbers to a formal mathematical treatment, and there is really nothing wrong with putting economic indicators into a mathematical framework (though we will discuss later the virtue of plain graphics as opposed to elaborate regressions). The idea, however, is that whatever is done to the numbers does not in and of itself guarantee better results—the math comes ahead of the

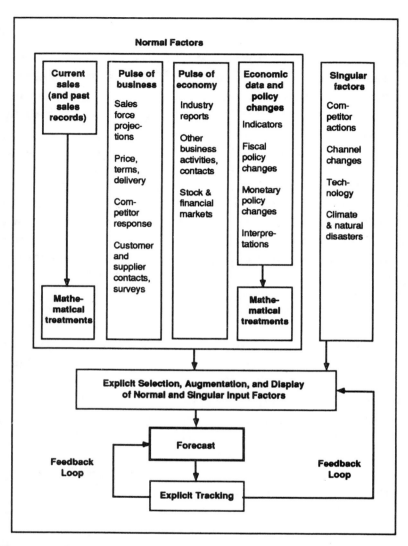

Figure 12-2. Forecasting components and process.

Better forecasting results mainly from greater attention to careful tracking of results, followed by modification of the methods used.

box called "Selection, Augmentation, and Display," ahead of synthesis into a forecast, and ahead of explicit tracking and feedback. In other words, the process of independent thought holds rank over the mathematics; the mind can say, yes, the crunching helped, or, no, the crunching hid the truth from us.

13

Tracking the Indicators

Making accurate economic forecasts begins with a straight-forward approach to selecting and displaying economic indicators. The key is for the executive to be directly involved in the process and to be responsible for its authenticity. If the executive is not willing to take a hands-on approach to tracking indicators and to formatting them in a usable, personalized fashion, then the benefits promised in this book will be considerably lessened.

The old name for the tracking exercise I recommend is *philology*, which to medieval scholars meant "the comparison of texts." How does one know that the data presented are really the data they are said to be? What changes have been made in the data as they are passed from originator to typesetter to first user to critic to interpreter and so on down the line? How can one be sure that the information is in its rawest form, with no causal connections added by other people?

An executive interested in U.S. housing starts should be sure to have the latest raw figures, as a first step, before accepting someone's interpretation of what the figures mean. Otherwise he or she will never be able to get disentangled from the econometric models into which housing figures are immediately put by most experts. Business leaders must try to deal directly with the figures in their own mind, without help, or with no more than clerical help, or else they will miss their best chance of beating their competition—through their own ability to forecast trends better than any economic model can possibly do.

The economic data exercise I am about to recommend is similar to starting up an accounting system. Suppose you sit down with a clean sheet of paper and begin to list what you want your controller to send you in the way of company performance data. You know what you want—a better and more immediate grasp of operational realities—and you know how it should look when it is done. Executives can and should exercise the same prerogative with their researchers. They should make a list of what they want to know about the economy and how the report should look when it is done properly.

Ask yourself, "What are the economic factors of most interest to me?" In posing the question, try to separate what you have been told by others to be interested in from what you yourself are interested in. "What stories in the paper catch my eye, time after time?" There will be a reason for this—your mind is looking for the things it needs to do its job, regardless of what your experts have been saying.

In making your list, remember that you are not trying to be

complete, the way an economist would mean "complete." You are not an empirical scientist attempting to capture the entire universe of published economic data and then be able to analyze them for the correct answer. This cannot be done anyway. There is no correct answer. It is okay to ignore factors that others seem to talk about a lot, providing that your honest appraisal is that those things have never helped you or interested you in the past, and provided that you are committed to the kind of honest feedback loop discussed in the previous chapter.

What you are trying to do here is to make yourself a tiny bit better than you already are at what you already do well. You are attempting to set up things to enable yourself to display your opinions and ideas, in the hope of finding errors, myths, omissions, contradictions, and areas for more careful study—all of which will push out your frontiers.

Ask yourself the question once again, "What are the economic factors of most interest to me?" Without consulting any text or asking anyone, make a list. Do not worry about exact names if you do not know them. Use slang for what you remember.

The next step is to go to the library and get the current issue of *Economic Indicators*, a monthly publication. This thirty-four-page document is prepared by the Council of Economic Advisers for the Joint Economic Committee of Congress and is printed by the Government Printing Office. It contains nothing beyond the purest numbers themselves, with a few graphs, and has no interpretive text. It is meant to be a handy collection of that economic data that members of Congress and bureaucrats most often want. It is by no means complete, especially not at the regional or international level.

Flip through *Economic Indicators* and examine the table of

contents. Try, without help, to find the items on your list. If it turns out that an indicator you want to follow is not in this publication, be aware that most other people, especially members of Congress (who affect your business mightily), are therefore probably not following it. If one of your items is not present, it is most likely (1) regional (state or city), (2) international, which Congress is weak at following, or (3) industry-specific, beyond the major categories of automobiles, steel, and housing. The process that you apply to regional, international, and industry-specific data is identical to what you should do when dealing with the national economy, except you will use publications other than *Economic Indicators*.

Let's go back to the list of economic factors of personal interest to you, and let's assume now that you have put aside those other than the ones dealing with the national economy. How long is the list? How long should it be? Let me be ridiculous at one extreme: If you listed a hundred things, that is too many. You are kidding yourself. I will not deny that the mind can handle a hundred things at once, but you will not be able to track that many in a data base without turning the job over to a computer model. The idea here is to not turn the job over. The idea is to do what is practical with data to improve your own mind, especially to bolster your skepticism, your ability to tell myth from fact. It would not be practical to keep track of a hundred factors.

At the other extreme, if your list had only two or three items, it is too short. I would grant you that most market decisions will hinge on mainly a couple of items, but this is usually after extensive debate has substantially narrowed down the starting list to the two or three things that are the hardest to determine.

As a starting point, I recommend a list that contains between five and nine items. Eventually your new data base might have the following:

1. Five to nine indicators on the national economy
2. Five to nine indicators on the international economy
3. Five to nine regional indicators
4. Five to nine industry-specific indicators

If you are managing a business with many divisions and many locations, then there may be more than a total of four sets of data, but I recommend erring on the side of too small rather than too big. It may be more appropriate for divisional or regional managers to set up and maintain the data than for the executive at headquarters to do it.

Set aside a couple of hours. Buy a data pad like that shown in Figure 13–1. The number of years to display and the sequence in which to put the indicators on your list are very, very important. In making the table for yourself, you are communicating to yourself what you really believe about how things work and how you can best follow events as they unfold and test your views. For instance, if you believe that interest rates cause everything, and GNP is a result, place interest rates in column 1 and GNP in column 7. Or if you think that the deficit is of primary importance, put it in column 1 and perhaps put interest rates next to it. If you think that everything starts with the confidence of people to produce, put GNP in column 1.

Arrange your factors on the national economy in some kind of order, even if it is somewhat arbitrary. You can change the order later. In fact, this is the key point: In the ever-evolving complexity of human affairs, some factors will come to the fore and others will recede. Your job is to be better than your competition at judging what is in column 1 today.

Let's say now you have a data pad that looks like Figure 13–2. You have not only selected a list of indicators but you have put them into a tentative order—and you have said, "I'm going to look several years back, at least to begin with."

The next task is to write in the numbers. This will not be as easy as it sounds. It is here that you will come up against the real value of this exercise for you. For the indicators on your list, which you may have expressed in general terms, you will now have to get specific, and you will have to choose between an indicator's total and its parts, between its base and its change, and between its unadjusted form and adjusted form. In most

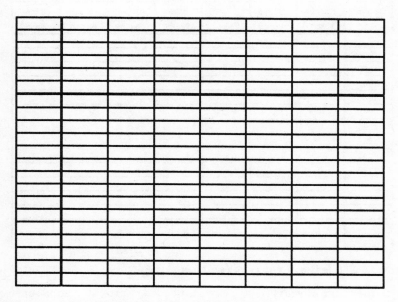

Figure 13-1. Blank data pad for tracking indicators.

Find a blank data pad with about eight columns—one for years, the others for your own selection of economic indicators.

cases, however, you will be able to find the form of the indicator that has been of interest to you in news stories. For instance, in GNP it is usually total and change; that is, U.S. total GNP grew at 6.8 percent in 1985, adjusted to 1972 dollars. In housing starts, it is total and base; that is, total U.S. housing starts were 1.8 million in 1985, seasonally adjusted. In prime interest rate, it

Calendar year	US merch-andise trade balance ($billion)	US GDP (1987$) percent change)	US budget deficit ($billion)	Fed money supply M-2 (percent change)	Con-sumer price index (percent change)	New home mortgage yield (percent)	New housing starts (thou-sand)
1981							
1982							
1983							
1984							
1985							
1986							
1987							
1988							
1989							
1990							
1991							

Figure 13-2. Selection of years and indicators.

Fill in the range of years that you feel is needed to provide a good sense of history and fill in the names of the indicators that interest you the most. The order of the indicators is important: Start at the upper left with the most important ones and move across the right toward the ones with the most impact on your particular business.

is total and base; that is, prime interest in 1985 was 10.2 percent as an unadjusted average.

At this point you will probably also become aware that annual figures are not enough to meet the pace of how often things in the economy change; you will want quarterly and in some cases monthly data. But for the moment, stick with annual figures.

Your data pad should now look like Figure 13–3, and you are ready to have a discussion with your researcher. (If you are

Calendar year	US merch- andise trade balance ($billion)	US GDP (1987$ percent change)	US budget deficit ($billion)	Fed money supply M-2 (percent change)	Con- sumer price index (percent change)	New home mortgage yield (percent)	New housing starts (thou- sand)
1981	15	1.8	-79			14.7	
1982	4	-2.2	-128	8.9	3.8	15.1	1062
1983	-30	3.9	-208	12.0	3.8	12.6	1703
1984	-86	6.2	-185	8.6	3.9	12.4	1750
1985	-107	3.2	-212	8.2	3.8	11.6	1742
1986	-129	2.9	-221	9.4	1.1	10.2	1805
1987	-146	3.1	-150	3.5	4.4	9.3	1621
1988	-111	3.9	-155	5.5	4.4	9.2	1488
1989	-91	2.5	-154	5.0	4.6	10.1	1376
1990	-70	1.0	-221	3.2	6.1	10.1	1193
1991		-0.7	-269	2.9	3.1	9.3	1015

Figure 13-3. Completed data base.

Complete your data base by using entries from *Economic Indicators* (or other sources). You can make your forecasts of 1992 directly on the above figure, or if you have a researcher to assist you, you may wish to augment the figure, as shown in Figure 13-4, including data on the months and quarters preceding your annual forecast.

your own researcher, so much the better. The kind of research to be assigned here will not require the Ph.D. in economics or any other subject.) If you have never designed such a data base, your researcher will certainly be impressed. He or she will see that you are serious and that you are willing to study the data in their raw form. Tell your researcher that you are providing a rough form of how you believe you could best follow the national economy; that you want the researcher to clean it up and add months and quarters; that you want to develop similar tables to international, regional, and industry-specific factors; and that you want the researcher to maintain them for you and give you regular updates. If all goes well, the researcher will supply you with a table such as that shown in Figure 13–4.

Once you start receiving clean versions of your own list of economic indicators, what do you do? What is the purpose of the whole exercise? You put down in your own hand, at the bottom of the table, your own forecasts of the future. You do this every time you get an updated table. Before you make a fresh forecast, however, you score how well you did on the last one. You check your projected figures against what the numbers actually became when released by the government. When you are wrong, you challenge your own arguments. Maybe you need to change the order of your factors, or maybe you are missing some factors that have now made themselves felt.

To whom does your copy of this table go, with your own forecast? My recommendation is to no one. In its details, it is between you and you. Whatever business decisions you are making in any given period of time will be affected, willy-nilly, by your forecast of the future, whether or not you have the kind of indicator tables I recommend. In other words, no business person is ever without a forecast. But very few of your competitors, even if a book like this were in wide circulation, will expend the effort to make their own forecasts visible to themselves, to enable their minds to improve.

Calendar year	US merch- andise trade balance ($billion)	US GDP (1987$ percent change)	US budget deficit ($billion)	Fed money supply M-2 (percent change)	Con- sumer price index (percent change)	New home mortgage yield (percent)	New housing starts (thou- sand)
1981	15	1.8	-79			14.7	
1982	4	-2.2	-128	8.9	3.8	15.1	1062
1983	-30	3.9	-208	12.0	3.8	12.6	1703
1984	-86	6.2	-185	8.6	3.9	12.4	1750
1985	-107	3.2	-212	8.2	3.8	11.6	1742
1986	-129	2.9	-221	9.4	1.1	10.2	1805
1987	-146	3.1	-150	3.5	4.4	9.3	1621
1988	-111	3.9	-155	5.5	4.4	9.2	1488
1989	-91	2.5	-154	5.0	4.6	10.1	1376
1990	-70	1.0	-221	3.2	6.1	10.1	1193
1991		-0.7	-269	2.9	3.1	9.3	1015
1992F							
	Season- ally adjusted	Season- ally adjusted		Season- ally adjusted	Month to month	Monthly	Season- ally adjusted
Jul				3.6	0.2	9.4	1049
Aug				2.3	0.2	9.5	1056
Sep				1.2	0.4	9.3	1017
91-III	-9	1.8					
Oct				1.2	0.1	9.0	1090
Nov				1.3	0.4	8.6	1075
Dec				1.4	0.3	8.5	1103
91-IV		0.3					

Figure 13-4. Data base augmented by researcher.

14

Correlations and Models

In both economics and business, frequent use is made of the mathematical concept of correlation. An economist might say, "There is a high correlation between growth of the country's GNP and the rate of corporate profits."

As shown in Figure 14–1, this correlation is indeed very strong. In periods of high growth of the country's GNP, corporate profits tend also to be high, and in periods of economic downturn, corporate profits are much weaker. The correlation, however, year by year, is not 100 percent—or as a mathematician might say, the correlation is not one-to-one.

The degree to which a correlation approaches a perfect fit can be measured mathematically and assigned a number between 0.00 and 1.00. This number is called the *correlation coefficient* of the

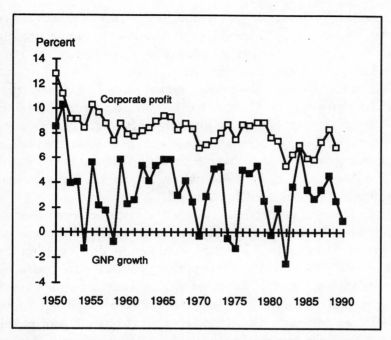

Figure 14-1. Growth in U.S. GNP versus corporate profits (before-tax profit of manufacturing companies stated as a percent of sales).

The profits of manufacturing companies, stated as a percent of sales, are higher than the growth of GNP and are somewhat less volatile. But the correlation is simple and strong, despite the fact that it does not hold for each and every year: The greater the growth in GNP, the greater the rate of corporate profits.

(Sources: Economic Indicators and Council of Economic Advisers, Economic Report of the President, various issues.)

relationship in question, and when the coefficient climbs above 0.90 or higher, the relationship is thought of as being more and more significant. The two lines in the graph of Figure 14–1 are correlated well above a coefficient of 0.90.

But what exactly does this mean? Does it mean that economic growth causes growth in corporate profits? And if so, does it mean that economic growth unfailingly causes such profits? And if this in turn is true, what happened in 1985 when economic growth lept to over 6 percent but profits increased only modestly? Or in 1974 when economic growth was negative but profits actually climbed?

In Chapter 4, in discussing the difference between models and reality, I made the point that, "In reality, there are no independent variables." What I meant is now illustrated in the case of economic growth and corporate profits. Neither variable is independently causal. In other words, they are much more codependent than independent. In times of high economic growth, we can generally anticipate that corporate profits will indeed be high, but this need not always be the case. Other factors can intervene. The publication of a GNP figure of 6 percent growth will not necessarily be followed by high corporate earnings figures. Nor will news of high profits guarantee a big positive boost in GNP. More is going on in the world of business and economics than just business and economics—for instance, politics, governmental actions, and a host of cultural and international affairs.

The correlation between economic growth and corporate profits is what we should think of as instructive but not dictatorial. Correlations teach some basic lessons in the structure of economic and business life, but the economist who systematically parses a hundred or a thousand data series such as the two shown in Figure 14–1 will find lots of good correlations but no strong predictability.

The way that economic indicators behave is like a family, or perhaps like a large herd of animals. Picture a herd of camels free to roam across a large desert. Suppose the camels all have names, like "Housing," "Factory Orders," "Inventories," "Retail Sales," and so forth. Now suppose that you fly above the herd in an airplane, watching the herd's movement. In all likelihood, the members of the herd will spread out for a while and then come back together, as they wander across the desert, making a path only in retrospect. The position of any one animal in the herd will be well correlated with the total of the other members of the herd; that is, the camels will all stick together, though at times some animals will be in front, some in the middle, and some in the back, and then vice versa. Certain of the camels may have a strong tendency usually to be in the front or the back. In fact, over a long period of time, the relative positions of each animal to all the others may become fairly consistent. But the question is, Can you use the known position of one (or a few) animals in the herd to predict where the whole herd will be tomorrow? Or next week? Or a year from now?

What chance of forecasting the future does a model of this kind have? How can a model be accurate that uses mathematical correlations (often called multiple regressions) to predict where the whole is going from an analysis of the parts?

SIMPLE MODELS, YES; COMPLEX MODELS, NO

Following a speech I once made on the above concepts, a business researcher objected not so much to my allegation that large models always fail but to my seeming criticism of the use of any model whatever. "Isn't everything a model?" the researcher asked. "What choice do we have besides models?'

The point was well taken. A simple model that helps to make clear the interaction of a few key forces is good. Graphs of the type shown in Figure 14–1 are good; they show the eye that two factors are well correlated, and they show the degree to which history can be expected to cast a similar pattern on the future.

My problem is with complex models that admit a multitude of forces and that turn over the ownership of causality to a set of simultaneous equations. This approach is not good. Since the user cannot clearly see how the forces are supposedly interacting, the user is left to trust that the mathematics have gotten it right—for which the only measure is how good the forecast is. And as we all know, when we put aside our wish that the method would work, econometric forecasts are a complete failure.

The key issue here is once again ownership. I claim that the best forecasts are made by the knowledgeable mind, assisted by regular tracking of the indicators and by live assessment of the overall environment in which economics and business are taking place. Such a mind wants and needs good, simple models—like the two-variable graph that plots the correlation of economic growth and corporate profits. But when the mind surrenders its own processing of the problem to an extrasomatic device (a device outside the body, such as a computer), the battle is lost. The mind is wishing that more certainty could be found than the world will allow, or the mind is wishing that something that is very hard could be made easy. But alas, the mind itself must do the hardest part, namely the perceiving of causal relationships and their synthesis into the most likely outcome. A computer may very well help to display the composition and structure of the major forces, as by graphing and charting, but a computer cannot substitute for the human mind via multiple regression (or expert systems, or neural networks, and so on.)

WHY COMPLEX MODELS SURVIVE

In my experience, the executive is more often responsible for the survival of complex models than the economist. What often happens is a competent executive, let's say in sales or marketing, begins to rise in his or her organization. The rise is based not only on the ability to make sales or to earn good margins but also to be able to anticipate where the business is headed, when the customers are going to buy and how much, and when the outlook is weak rather than strong. After a few promotions, the executive finds himself or herself not so directly in touch with the market as before, due to the press of keeping dozens of other people doing what they should be doing. The reports of the pulse of business activity are now secondhand. It becomes more difficult for the executive to have an accurate outlook, in the fashion that he or she might formerly have called "automatic" or "natural." In addition, the economy itself may have taken an unusual turn, or the price of a key raw material may have skyrocketed.

At this point, the executive looks for assistance. What he or she remembers is that the outlook used to be easier to come by than now, and the factors that he or she followed were not innumerable, but rather they were simple. Why not have somebody in the organization track these market forces carefully and then help make the projections? The forces were all pretty logical, or so it seemed. Why not gain a competitive edge by putting together a better model of the market than the competition?

And now the cultural myths of economics as a science and of business strategy as a purely logical activity cut in, and all is eventually lost. The executive turns over control of the monitoring and forecasting to someone besides himself or herself—it need not be to an economist—and the process eventually culminates by the executive presenting someone else's forecasts (those of the best experts that money can buy) to the board, and both the executive and the board pretend to believe each other.

15

Nondistorting Graphs

The delineation of trends requires using graphs, and the methods of graphing are usually taught under the heading of "Cartesian Coordinates" in high school geometry. After that, formal education in the matter stops—even Ph.D. programs in which graphing is of central importance, such as economics, offer no special training in how to construct good graphs. There are proper ways to graph trends, and there are ways in which graphs may be used to illustrate the existence of trends that are not actually present and to grossly exaggerate ones that are.

An example of a properly prepared graph is shown in Figure 15–1. The subject matter is U.S. new housing starts and the issue is whether the trend is on an upswing or a downswing.

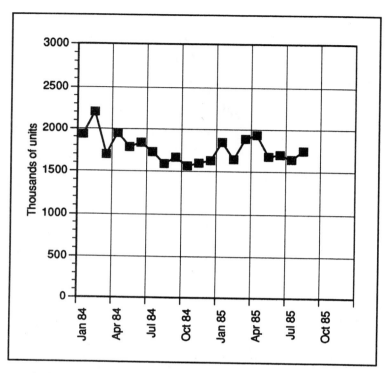

Figure 15-1. U.S. new housing starts.

This figure, compared to Figures 15-2 through 15-5, shows the proper way to graph eighteen months of data on housing starts. The *y*-axis begins at 0, the trend line itself is positioned in the middle of a square grid, and the *x*-axis extends beyond the final data point.

(Source: Economic Indicators.)

The time frame is twenty-four months. To prepare a graph like the one in Figure 15–1, follow these rules:

1. Use line graphs, not bar graphs or other types.
2. Use axes of approximately equal length to result in a square, not rectangular, grid.
3. Always begin the y-axis at zero when displaying the magnitude of an indicator.
4. Extend the y-axis far enough so that the trend line itself is approximately centered in the coordinate field.
5. Extend the x-axis well beyond the final data point.
6. Always plot grid lines, both horizontal and vertical ones. Size the grid so that there are ten grid lines (plus or minus two), both horizontally and vertically.

The conclusion I would draw from looking at the graph in Figure 15–1 is that housing starts are relatively stable; perhaps, but not certainly, they bottomed out in October 1984. If I wanted to illustrate this conclusion more forcefully, and I did not care about objectivity, I would graph it as shown in Figure 15–2. In flattening out the square frame, I have flattened the trend line itself. Rectangular graphs do this whether you want it done or not.

Someone who disagrees with my conclusion of stability in housing starts could provide Figure 15–3. By chopping off the y-axis and not showing its zero-point, the changes are emphasized—and a downwardness over the whole eighteen months is also introduced.

A bar chart with y-axis and x-axis foreshortened emphasizes volatility, as demonstrated in Figure 15–4. Figure 15–5 uses vertical rectangularity of the graph's framework to emphasize upwardness.

Changing a graph's framework literally changes the framework of the analysis. A person who chops off the *y*-axis so that small changes are easier to see is guided either consciously or unconsciously by a belief that small changes make a difference. Maybe they do, but maybe they do not.

If you change the axis of a graph to magnify small changes, you must be prepared to *own* the importance you thus give to the magnification. *You* are adding the weight, not the data themselves.

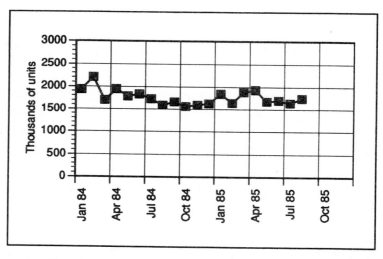

Figure 15-2. U.S. new housing starts.

Compared to Figure 15-1, this graph is improper—that is, it introduces distortions. Flattening the square grid into a rectangle also flattens the trend line, making the slope difficult to see.

(Source: Economic Indicators.)

When you see a graph that violates the rules of objective
graphing, the graph's author may have deliberately distorted
the material or may have done so accidentally. Generally
speaking, those who draw graphs so that you are forced to
focus on change instead of magnitude believe in the econometric
approach. Their models depend on tiny changes in the indicators,
fed through multiple-correlation equations. It will not seem
dishonest to them to show you graphs that are distorting the
truth.

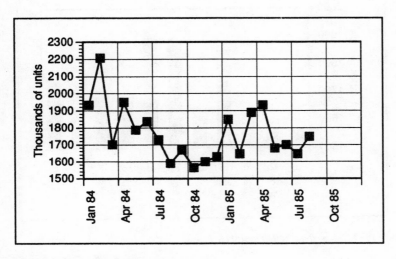

Figure 15-3. U.S. new housing starts.

In this improper graph, the *y*-axis does not start at 0, which magnifies
the variability of the data.

(Source: Economic Indicators.)

If you believe that change is indeed more important than magnitude, then I recommend a graphing procedure that clearly identifies your approach. Figure 15–6 illustrates this method. For the time period of interest—which must be chosen by the analyst, as it will not be chosen automatically by the data—calculate the average (or the slope of the trend, if it is clearly present). Then express each monthly figure in terms of a deviation from that average. For instance, in the case of our present example, the average monthly number of housing

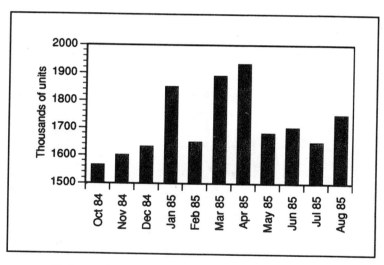

Figure 15-4. U.S. new housing starts.

This improper graph is a column chart in which the y-axis is fore-shortened and the x-axis is clipped of several months; it gives a different view of the trend by exaggerating month-to-month increases.

(Source: Economic Indicators.)

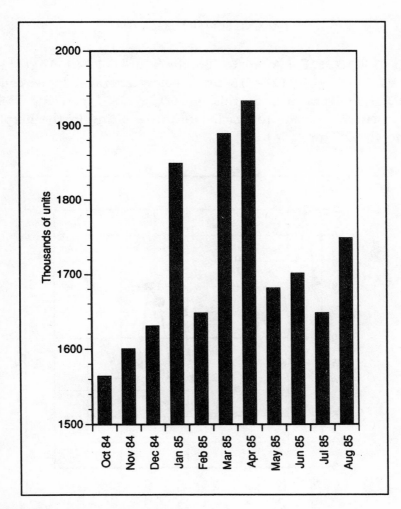

Figure 15-5. U.S. new housing starts.

This improper graph squeezes the data into a vertical rectangle that introduces an upward bias to the trend chart not apparent in another view of the same data.

(Source: Economic Indicators.)

starts is 1,765. For August 1985, the figure is 1,749. August is thus 1,765 − 1,749 = 16 units below average. In percent deviation from average this is 16/1,765 = 1 percent. This calculation is made for each month, resulting in the graph shown in Figure 15–6.

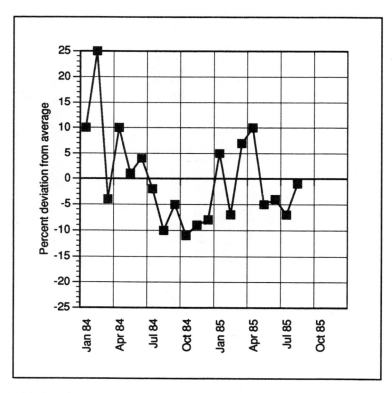

Figure 15-6. Changes in U.S. new housing starts.

The proper way to display changes in monthly data is as a percent deviation from the average (or trend).

(Source: Economic Indicators.)

NONDISTORTING GRAPHS

Now suppose that you suspect that changes in housing starts are affected by changes in home mortgage interest rates. You find a monthly indicator for mortgages rates, calculate the percent deviation from the average over the same period used for housing starts, and display the two lines as shown in Figure 15–7.

What can be concluded from Figure 15–7? (1) Upward changes in mortgages rates tend to be associated with downward changes in housing starts, but with notable exceptions. (2) Housing starts in May, June, and July of 1985 were down from the average despite lower mortgage rates. Were loan standards changed? Did prospective housing buyers spend money on something else? Was disposable income less?

The value of Figure 15–7 is that you can see the extent of reliability in the common assertion that as interest rates fall, housing starts increase. "All other things being equal," an economist might say. If, however, the same economist went on to model all the other factors that affect housing, and then proceeded to say that a particular one had a particular effect, I would certainly disagree.

Mathematics and graphing will not allow you to harness the universe. No variables are truly independent. You cannot make "all other things equal." You can only recast one problem in terms of another. But seeing an old problem in a new fresh way is often worth lots of money to us, especially if we see it before our competitors do.

One final caveat about Figure 15–7. The base of housing numbers is four digits (for example, 1,765; 1,820; and so on), whereas the base of mortgage rates is only two digits (12.5 percent, 11.9 percent, and so on). When this disparity in bases is present, there will often be a disparity in the percent change as well. But this should not be taken to mean that one indicator is

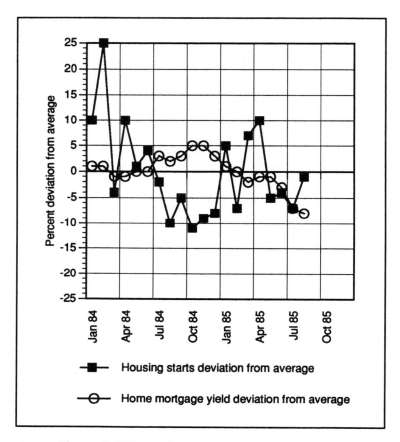

Figure 15-7. Changes in U.S. new housing starts versus changes in mortgage rates.

This figure shows the proper way to display changes in order to see whether two factors are correlated. In this case, upward moves of mortgage rates are often, but not always, associated with downward moves in housing starts.

(Source: Economic Indicators.)

either more or less volatile than the other. The reason is in the nature of percentages themselves: When I am one-year old and become two, my age is 100 percent greater; yet when I am ten-years old and become eleven, my age is only 10 percent greater. The size of the base affects the calculation of percentages, and it cannot be escaped in the presentation of results. Presentation is of equal importance to analysis. Graphic distortion costs society perhaps billions of dollars every year.

16

Tracking the Domestic Business Cycle

Over the past several decades, the U.S. economy has alternated between periods of strong (or fairly strong) economic growth and shorter periods of economic decline. In the 1950s and 1960s, the patterns of growth and decline were more regular than they became in the 1970s and 1980s, as the domestic economy became more and more affected by international competition. And as the years went by, economists produced dozens upon dozens of different models to explain the periodicity in the U.S. economy, with the hope of predicting the strength and timing of the next upturn or downturn. None of these methods have worked.

It is nonetheless completely true that the U.S. economy cycles between positive growth and negative growth (that is, decline), and it is equally clear that the ability to foresee this pattern would be extremely valuable to business—in terms of the timing of inventory buildups, new product introduction, factory capacity enlargement or reduction, and other aspects of business strategy.

In acknowledging that the domestic economy has ups and downs, and in calling these *cycles,* I am by no means supporting the mythical view that the timing of the economy's periods is determined by some preordained rhythm in human affairs. Instead, I am saying that since the future cannot be accurately predicted, the next best thing to do is to monitor its unfolding better than one's competitors.

The technique I recommend is to adopt a common model of the cycle and track the data that support the model in a way that makes its very ambiguity and inconclusiveness clear. Tracking of this kind will help the executive to claim full ownership of his or her own view of where the domestic economy stands, to discuss the view with others, and to break the myth that some kind of mechanical laws lie beneath the economy's motion.

In his book, *Guide to Using the Wall Street Journal,*[1] M. Lehman describes four phases in the domestic business cycle.

1. Trough to recovery
2. Recovery to expansion
3. Expansion to peak
4. Peak to contraction

These four phases are shown diagrammatically in Figure 16–1. It is not possible to be very precise about when one phase begins and another phase ends. The phases can be monitored, however, by the ups and downs in various economic indicators that are grouped according to the two main sides of economic activity—that is, the supply side and the demand side.

In this model, the supply side of the economy is made up of

GNP, industrial production, factory capacity utilization, productivity, and producer prices. If all of these indicators are up in the month or quarter of interest, then the economy is said to be in phase 3 above, expansion to peak. If all of these indicators are down, then the economy is in phase 1 above, trough to recovery.

The demand side in this model is made up of such indicators as the consumer price index, consumer real income, consumer confidence, and consumer demand (the components of which can be automobile sales, consumer credit, retail sales, housing

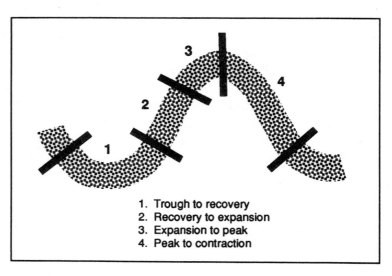

1. Trough to recovery
2. Recovery to expansion
3. Expansion to peak
4. Peak to contraction

Figure 16-1. Phases in the domestic business cycle.

These divisions of the cycle are qualitative and essentially arbitrary. Economists have developed many dozens of ways to characterize the ups and downs of economic growth.

(Source: Adapted from M. Lehman, The Dow Jones-Irwin Guide to Using the Wall Street Journal, New York: Warner Books, 1982.)

starts, and so on). If all of the demand side indicators are up, then the economy is in phase 2 above, recovery to expansion. If all of the demand side indicators are down, then the economy is in phase 4 above, peak to contraction.

The structure of the phases and the direction of the various members of the family of indicators is shown in Table 16–1.

Table 16–1 Phases in the Domestic Business Cycle Versus Change in Various Indicators

| | Phase of the Domestic Business Cycle | | | |
| | #1 Trough to Recovery | #2 Recovery to Expansion | #3 Expansion to Peak | #4 Peak to Contraction |
Indicators				
Supply-side indicators				
Is GNP up?	no		yes	
Is industrial production up?	no		yes	
Is capacity utilization up?	no		yes	
Is productivity down?	no		yes	
Are producer prices up?	no		yes	
Demand-side indicators				
Is CPI down?		yes		no
Is consumer real income up?		yes		no
Is consumer confidence up?		yes		no
Is consumer demand up?		yes		no
Auto sales up?		yes		no
Consumer credit up?		yes		no
Retail sales up?		yes		no
Housing starts up?		yes		no

If growth in the above set of indicators was always uniform, then determination of what phase the economy is in would be easy to determine. But in reality, the growth pattern is always mixed.

	Industrial Production (total)		
Period	% Change from year earlier	Is production down?	Is production up?
1980	-1.9		
1981	1.9		
1982	-4.4		
1983	3.7		
1984	9.3		
1985	1.7		
1986	1.0		
1987	4.9		
1988	5.4		
1989	2.6		
1990			
90-Qtr-3			
Oct	2.0	yes	no
Nov	0.2	yes	no
Dec	-1.3	yes	no
90-Qtr-4			
Jan	-0.8	yes	no
Feb	-2.6	yes	no
Mar	-3.6	yes	no
91-Qtr-1			
Apr	-3.0	no	yes
May	-2.7	no	yes
Jun	-2.5	no	yes
91-Qtr-2			
Jul	-2.2	no	yes
Aug	-2.0	no	yes
Sep	-2.2	yes	no

The real benefit of this technique is not so much the model itself as the actual tracking of economic data it requires. A sample table of how to track a single indicator is shown in Figure 16–2. Not only must the executive find and enter the actual numbers but he or she must make the decision as to whether the indicator is up or down from the previous period. Such a determination may seem easy, but since the indicators are always revised and re-revised, the task becomes both demanding and informative. As shown in the figure, the user puts a "yes" and a "no" in the columns opposite the data entries, and then carries these qualitative words forward to Figure 16–3.

At this point, with all the "yes's" and "no's" in one big table, the executive can pull back and attempt to gain an overview of the economy's position in the domestic cycle. If the table shows mostly "yes's," then the economy is probably in expansion. If the table shows mostly "no's," then the economy may well be in decline. Examine the difference, for instance, in the early quarters of 1990, when "yes's" predominate, and the October–November–December period of 1990, when "no's" begin to take over.

Figure 16-2. Sample data setup for tracking a single indicator's growth ("yes–no").

This setup must be kept for each of the fifteen factors to be used in the domestic business cycle model of Figure 16-1and Table 16-1. Information is available from such publications as the monthly *Economic Indicators* (U.S. Government Printing Office).

---

	90 Qtr-3	90 Oct	90 Nov	90 Dec	90 Qtr-4	91 Jan	91 Feb	91 Mar	91 Qtr-1	91 Apr	91 May	91 Jun	91 Qtr-2
All "yes" = Expansion to Peak (#3)													
All "no" = Trough to Recovery (#1)													
Is GNP up?	no				no				yes				yes
Is industrial production up?		no	no	no		no	no	no		yes	yes	yes	
Is capacity utilization up?		no	no	no		no	no	no		yes	yes	yes	
Is productivity down?	yes				no				no				no
Are producer prices up?		yes	yes	no		no	no	no		yes	yes	yes	
All "yes" = Recovery to Expansion (#2)													
All "no" = Peak to Contraction (#4)													
Is CPI down?		no	no	yes		yes	yes	yes		no	no	yes	
Is consumer real income up?	yes				no				no				yes
Is consumer confidence up?		no	no	no		no	yes	yes		no	no	yes	
Is consumer demand up?	yes				no				no				yes
Auto sales up?	yes				no				no				yes
Consumer credit up?		no	yes	no		no	yes	no		yes	no	no	
Retail sales up?		no	yes	no		no	yes	yes		no	yes	no	
Housing starts up?		no	yes	no		no	yes	no		yes	yes	yes	

Figure 16–3. Sample for displaying all "yes–no" data at once.

Notice how the supply-side indicators (the top five) shift from mainly "no's" in the last quarter of 1990 to "yes's" in early 1991. But the demand-side indicators stay mixed in both periods, illustrating the difficulty of determining the exact state of the economy until well after the fact.

But the principal message from the "yes–no" table is that it is almost always a mixed message. This is not, in my view, a defect in the quality of the model, but a simple reflection of truth in today's complex reality. The world economy, with our domestic economy as a key constituent (sometimes leading, sometimes not), is under no universal obligation to behave in a neat and tidy fashion.

The reader who applies the straightforward method given here and who comes to understand that elaborate, interlocking equations cannot link the family of indicators any better than his or her own eye, scanning Figure 16–3 for an overall pattern, has indeed come a very long way in owning the inherent uncertainty of reality, and in equipping himself or herself to beat the competition by slightly better forecasts, made slightly ahead of the herd.

17

Using "Bubble Charts" in Forecasting

Throughout the third part of this book, in presenting a number of methods that have worked for me in making better forecasts, my emphasis has been on simplicity, regularity, explicitness, and, in the end, ownership of procedures by the mind of the executive seeking a new avenue to competitive advantage. The methods I prefer can be executed mainly with paper and pencil, or with a personal computer if the reader prefers—though none of the techniques requires advanced mathematics.

My approach to better forecasting is in the same spirit as the method recommended by Benjamin Franklin for making better decisions. In a 1772 letter to his friend Joseph Priestly, Franklin said:

> I cannot, for want of sufficient premises, advise you *what* to determine, but if you please I will tell you *how*. . . . My way is to divide half a sheet of paper by a line into two columns; writing over the one *Pro*, and over the other *Con*. Then, during three or four days' consideration, I put down under the different heads short hints of the different motives, that at different times occur to me *for* or *against* the measure. When I have thus got them all together in one view, I endeavor to estimate the respective weights . . . [to] find at length where the balance lies . . . and, though the weight of reasons cannot be taken with the precision of algebraic quantities, yet, when each is thus considered, separately and comparatively, and the whole matter lies before me, I think I can judge better, and am less liable to make a rash step; and in fact I have found great advantage for this kind of equation, in what may be called *moral* or *prudential algebra*.

Franklin's idea of "prudential algebra" can be applied to the weighting and analysis of your own personal economic forecasts. The examples in this chapter are taken from my own forecast for GNP growth in 1990 that I made in December of the previous year.

First, list all of the factors you believe will affect the economy in the coming period. Second, rank the factors by importance, on a scale from 0 to 10. Third, rate the factors according to their potential impact on the economy, either positive or negative. Fourth, combine the ranking and the rating into one single display, so that in Franklin's words, you have "got them all together in one view."

Figure 17–1 shows my list of factors on a grid. Figure 17–2 shows my weighting of the factors by their importance and my

Factor							
Soviet economic restructuring (perestroika)							
Eastern Europe opening to West							
Decline of U.S. defense budget							
China's pullback from market economy							
Int'l demand for manufactured goods							
Stronger dollar from political uncertainty							
Increasing diversity of U.S. & int'l economy							
Improved U.S. productivity, competitiveness							
Cycle psychology of business, investors							
Market disillusion with LBOs, junk bonds							
Stock market volatility							
Gramm-Rudman cutback of gov't spending							
Environmentalism							
Demographics (less housing, more savings)							

Figure 17-1. First step in making a complex conclusion by means of a bubble chart.

Step 1. Make an exhaustive list of factors. In this example, the goal is to forecast U.S. GNP in 1990. Start with the grid pad and make a list of all the factors you can think of that may affect the strangth of the country's economic output in the coming year. At this stage, try to be complete without ranking the factors.

setting up of the grid to make a rating of impact on 1990 GNP. Figure 17–3 shows my rating of all fourteen factors. In Figure 17–4, I have converted the "x's" of the previous figure to numerical values by entering the weighting of importance from Figure 17–2 into the grid at the places where I had made the

Wt.	Factor	U.S. GNP IN 1990						
		Down						Up
		-3	-2	-1	0	1	2	3
3	Soviet economic restructuring (perestroika)							
4	Eastern Europe opening to West							
2	Decline of U.S. defense budget							
1	China's pullback from market economy							
3	Int'l demand for manufactured goods							
2	Stronger dollar from political uncertainty							
3	Increasing diversity of U.S. & int'l economy							
2	Improved U.S. productivity, competitiveness							
4	Cycle psychology of business, investors							
2	Market disillusion with LBOs, junk bonds							
2	Stock market volatility							
1	Gramm-Rudman cutback of gov't spending							
4	Environmentalism							
1	Demographics (less housing, more savings)							

Figure 17-2. Second step in making a complex conclusion by means of a bubble chart.

Step 2. On the grid pad, draw the framework of the problem, with several possible outcomes (seven such degrees are usually about right) for U.S. GNP in 1990—arranged on a scale from down (in this case −3 at the left) to up (in this case +3 on the right). Now assign a weight to each factor down the left column, capturing your feel of how important each one will be in the final outcome. For the factor weights, use a scale of 1 to 4. Least weight =1, most weight =4.

"x's." Figure 17–5 shows one way of displaying the final results, with penciled dots, and Figure 17–6 shows another way, using a personal computer to make proportionate circles.

The net result of my forecast was for a slight downturn in 1990, which of course turned out to be the right direction. In December 1989, of course, I could not foresee the Persian Gulf

Wt.	Factor	U.S. GNP IN 1990						
		Down						Up
		-3	-2	-1	0	1	2	3
3	Soviet economic restructuring (perestroika)					x		
4	Eastern Europe opening to West						x	
2	Decline of U.S. defense budget			x				
1	China's pullback from market economy			x				
3	Int'l demand for manufactured goods					x		
2	Stronger dollar from political uncertainty			x				
3	Increasing diversity of U.S. & int'l economy					x		
2	Improved U.S. productivity, competitiveness					x		
4	Cycle psychology of business, investors			x				
2	Market disillusion with LBOs, junk bonds			x				
2	Stock market volatility			x				
1	Gramm-Rudman cutback of gov't spending			x				
4	Environmentalism		x					
1	Demographics (less housing, more savings)				x			

Figure 17-3. Third step in making a complex conclusion by means of a bubble chart.

Step 3. Now put an "X" for each factor's probable impact on U.S. GNP in 1990, showing how you believe the factor will influence the outcome.

War or its consequences. In December 1989, too, I was apparently somewhat euphoric over the fall of the Berlin Wall and the opening of Eastern Europe toward the West—surely I should have known better than to have expected any kind of immediate payback, and instead I should have rated those factors on the downside of the matrix. This kind of mistake in

Wt.	Factor	U.S. GNP IN 1990						
		Down						Up
		-3	-2	-1	0	1	2	3
3	Soviet economic restructuring (perestroika)					3		
4	Eastern Europe opening to West						4	
2	Decline of U.S. defense budget			2				
1	China's pullback from market economy			1				
3	Int'l demand for manufactured goods					3		
2	Stronger dollar from political uncertainty			2				
3	Increasing diversity of U.S. & int'l economy					3		
2	Improved U.S. productivity, competitiveness					2		
4	Cycle psychology of businessmen, investors			4				
2	Market disillusion with LBOs, junk bonds			2				
2	Stock market volatility			2				
1	Gramm-Rudman cutback of gov't spending			1				
4	Environmentalism		4					
1	Demographics (less housing, more savings)				1			
	Overall		4	14	1	11	4	

Figure 17-4. Fourth step in making a complex conclusion by means of a bubble chart.

Step 4. Erase your "X's" from the third step and put in the number for the factor's weight from the left-hand column. Add the columns into an overall conclusion at the bottom (which in this example shows a leaning toward a downturn in 1990 GNP).

Wt.	Factor	U.S. GNP IN 1990						
		Down						Up
		-3	-2	-1	0	1	2	3
3	Soviet economic restructuring (perestroika)					••		
4	Eastern Europe opening to West						••	
2	Decline of U.S. defense budget			••				
1	China's pullback from market economy			•				
3	Int'l demand for manufactured goods					••		
2	Stronger dollar from political uncertainty			••				
3	Increasing diversity of U.S. & int'l economy					••		
2	Improved U.S. productivity, competitiveness					••		
4	Cycle psychology of business, investors			••				
2	Market disillusion with LBOs, junk bonds			••				
2	Stock market volatility			••				
1	Gramm-Rudman cutback of gov't spending			•				
4	Environmentalism		••					
1	Demographics (less housing, more savings)				•			
	Overall		••	•••	•	•••	••	

Figure 17-5. Fifth and final step in making a complex conclusion by means of a bubble chart.

Step 5. Displaying results. If you like, replace the numbers in the grid by an equivalent number of dots. This allows your eye to see the pattern of your weighting without having to read and interpret the numbers.

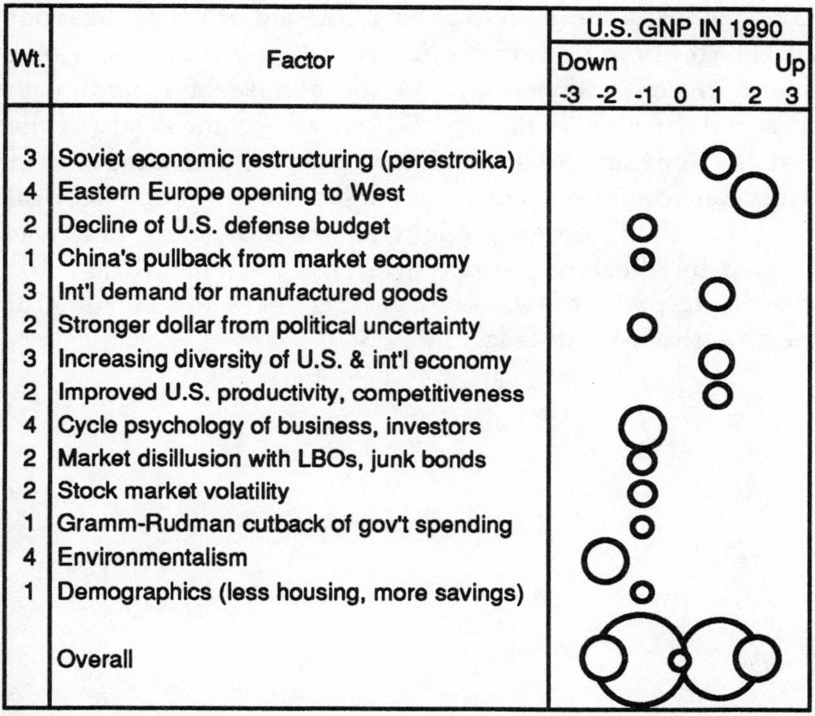

Wt.	Factor	U.S. GNP IN 1990 Down · · · · · · Up -3 -2 -1 0 1 2 3
3	Soviet economic restructuring (perestroika)	
4	Eastern Europe opening to West	
2	Decline of U.S. defense budget	
1	China's pullback from market economy	
3	Int'l demand for manufactured goods	
2	Stronger dollar from political uncertainty	
3	Increasing diversity of U.S. & int'l economy	
2	Improved U.S. productivity, competitiveness	
4	Cycle psychology of business, investors	
2	Market disillusion with LBOs, junk bonds	
2	Stock market volatility	
1	Gramm-Rudman cutback of gov't spending	
4	Environmentalism	
1	Demographics (less housing, more savings)	
	Overall	

Figure 17-6. Alternative final step in making a complex conclusion by means of a bubble chart.

Alternate Step 5. If you like using a desktop computer, you can "clean up" the dots in Figure 17-5 using proportional circles.

the big picture is common to us all, I'm afraid, and it exposes not only the role of our emotions in forecasting but our ignorance of both reality and history. As the demise of communism proceeded through 1990 and 1991, we all became aware of the great damage that had taken place to the productive capacity of the former communist countries, and of how a good historical analog for their recovery might be the slow pace that was followed by Western Europe after the Second World War. Recovery to prewar levels took several years and meaningful new growth took a decade.

18

Irreverence and Skepticism

The Federal Reserve, despite its enormous staff of Ph.D. economists, cannot foresee the turns in the economy any better than you or I can. As with many of the observations I have made, there is a double twist to this idea: The Fed is charged with forecasting the economy and with assuring the release of appropriate supplies of money to make the forecast come true. Therefore, despite the presence of absolute uncertainty, what the Fed thinks about the economy and what the Fed does with money supply and interest rates matter greatly to our own forecasting ability.

If in fact the reader had to choose only one focus for his or her study of economic opinion and outlook, it should be the Fed. The Fed's view will not be right, but the Fed's view will certainly matter. This double insight is a key element of better fore-casting. To beat our competition at forecasting, we must each become a better "Fed watcher" than our amateur counterparts in other companies.

PARALLEL PROCESSES

The most irreverent scheme I ever launched in the pursuit of better forecasting had to do with trying to better understand the Federal Reserve. The method is a branch of the discipline now called experimental economics, in which people play roles in a game that mimics some real economic process. In the case of my "parallel Fed," I sought to imitate the process the real Fed uses to set the level of pressure on bank reserves and thus to influence short-term interest rates. The real Fed meets as a group every six weeks to assess the economy and to issue an order to the New York Fed (the lead bank in carrying out monetary policy) as to whether bank reserves should be tightened or loosened. The Fed's decision-making group is called the Open Market Committee and it consists of seven Washington governros and five presidents from the Fed's twelve regional banks.

The kernel for my "mock Fed" came in 1984 from one of the real Fed governors, who was then president of the Boston Fed. He told me that while the Fed was proud of its economics research ("The best in the world, but I don't always understand it"), what really mattered was the pulse of the economy brought into the meeting by the regional presidents. Each regional president of a Fed bank has a board of governors made up of prominent businesspeople in the district and these leaders will commonly tell the Fed president exactly what is happening, or not, with their order books.

I thought that I could assemble a group of businesspeople and bankers and do the same thing as the real Fed. I found a couple of dozen willing volunteers and we began meeting on the same day as the real Fed's Open Market Committee. We followed the same basic approach as described in the Fed's minutes,* except in abbreviated form—that is, instead of a half-day's study of economic indicators and models, we spent a half-hour. Instead of a full day's debate on what decision to take, we took an hour.

But the outcome was both informative and competitive. I know of no better way to achieve a good track record in forecasting economic activity, interest rates, and other market factors—for a period of six weeks ahead—than the parallel process just described. The vote taken by the group of amateur governors was not the same thing as a quick survey of opinion. By participating in the meeting, each amateur found himself or herself actually playing the role of real governors and thus of owning what should be done as well as what will likely happen.

The forecast of the group of amateurs was published for all the members to use and the best form of consensus was that of a "bubble chart" of the major market factors, as shown in Figure 18–1. Notice how the technique allows an overview of GNP, inflation, exchange rates, trade volume, crude oil price, the stock market, interest rates, and the likely action of the Fed— simultaneously. Whether or not you initiate or become part of a parallel process, you should certainly try to pull together your overall outlook in this fashion, perhaps using the published

---

*The Fed's minutes are required reading for any executive wanting to improve his or her economic forecasts. The minutes of any given meeting are released three days after the next meeting, which means that they are about seven weeks old, but they are nonetheless a big tip-off about how the Fed thinks and what factors it considers important.

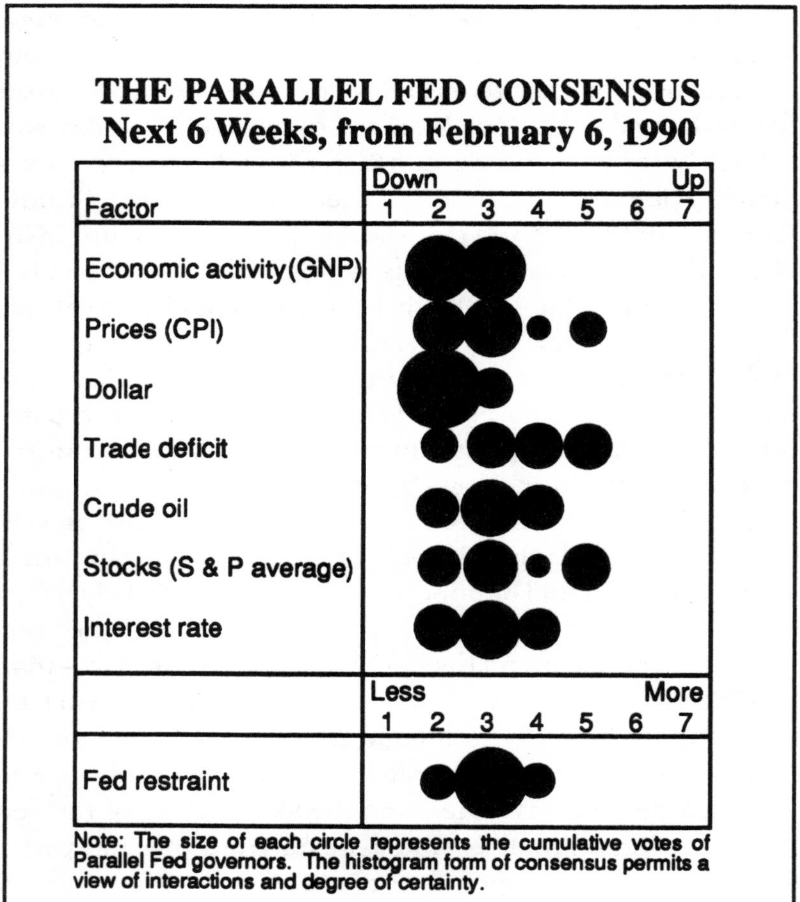

THE PARALLEL FED CONSENSUS
Next 6 Weeks, from February 6, 1990

Factor	Down 1 2 3 4 5 6 7 Up
Economic activity (GNP)	
Prices (CPI)	
Dollar	
Trade deficit	
Crude oil	
Stocks (S & P average)	
Interest rate	
	Less 1 2 3 4 5 6 7 More
Fed restraint	

Note: The size of each circle represents the cumulative votes of Parallel Fed governors. The histogram form of consensus permits a view of interactions and degree of certainty.

Figure 18-1. Sample consensus by bubble chart.

The direction of seven or eight different factors can be seen at one time, along with the dispersion of opinion about the direction. For instance, whereas opinion is uniform about the dollar, opinion is divided about the trade deficit and the stock market.

opinions of experts and/or the informal opinions of colleagues as your other governors.

PRIVATE SKEPTICISM

It is not necessary to go public with one's irreverence, but it is necessary to have and exercise strong skepticism about economics news, commentary, and interpretation. Most of the news is not really new, most of the commentary is by journalists who have not themselves been tracking the data, and most of the interpretation is political.

Skepticism is the great virtue of the mind to take in what someone else says, hold it as possibly true, and then subject it to objective reasoning. Skepticism is especially valuable in confronting the great economic myths of the present day, such as the belief that energy is running out, oil prices will always rise, and the U.S. trade balance will remain perpetually in the hole.

In the *Wall Street Journal*, a short column appeared by Lawrence B. Lindsey, called "America's Growing Economic Lead."[1] Articles taking the opposite view of the prevailing consensus always get my attention and in this case the author had only a few months earlier been appointed to the U.S. Federal Reserve Board—in my book a double cause for careful reading.

Mr. Lindsey's argument in favor of a growing lead for America was based on the growing strength of American manufactured exports in the 1990s as compared to the 1960s. In 1991, for instance, according to Mr. Lindsey, U.S. exports of capital goods amounted to 4 percent of U.S. gross domestic product (GDP), whereas in the late 1960s this figure for exports of capital goods was only 1.4 percent. Mr. Lindsey's recitation of the facts showed that U.S. strength in capital goods exports had tripled.

After reading the article, I sought more information. I was surprised that such an index as capital goods exports as a percent of GDP had tripled over the years without receiving any headlines, and taking Mr. Lindsey at his word for the moment, I was curious as to when the turnaround took place. In short, before I would adopt the good news as part of my continually changing worldview, I wanted to graph the numbers.

From standard sources,* I was able to construct the ratio mentioned in Mr. Lindsey's article. By my calculations, the share of GDP held by capital goods exports was 3 percent in 1991, not 4 percent as claimed by Mr. Lindsey, and the same number in the late 1960s was 1.2 percent or 1.3 percent, not 1.6 percent. Nonetheless the tripling was there in either set of data. I made a note to write a letter to Mr. Lindsey, asking for his data sources, but to adopt the basic conclusion he urged.

Furthermore, in following the urgings of my skepticism a little further, I found that I really had to reconstruct my entire attitude about how well the United States, at the end of 1991, was actually doing in world trade, and therefore about how competitive the country actually was—regardless of the political and journalistic rhetoric.

---

*Surprisingly few sources are needed by the serious reader in pursuit of monitoring the indicators and graphing history. The first requisite is *Economic Indicators*, published each month by the president's Council of Economic Advisers (CEA) for the use of Congress and other interested parties. Series reported in major newspapers but not in *Economic Indicators* can almost always be found in the *Survey of Current Business*, published monthly (and at a nominal charge) by the U.S. Department of Commerce. Finally, the annual *Economic Report of the President*, also published by the CEA, contains about a hundred pages of historical data on the U.S. economy in a most handy appendix.

Let us consider here the facts about trade as I rebuilt them following the urgings of the newest governor of the Fed. In focusing on trade, let us recognize that trade is by no means the only indicator of national competitiveness or well-being, but that it is the one most talked about. And what all the journalists have been saying about U.S. trade is that we have a big deficit, that it is getting worse, and that it is incurable.

But is this really true? Examine the accompanying charts in Figure 18–2. As can be seen in Figure 18–2, the U.S. merchandise trade balance is not getting worse—it is getting much

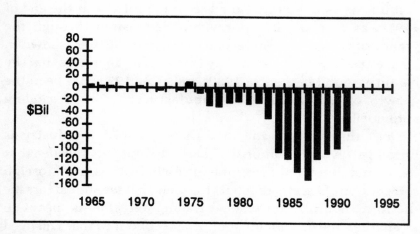

Figure 18-2. U.S. merchandise trade balance.

The big news about the U.S. trade balance at the end of 1991 was its improvement. The big reason for this, as shown in Figure 18-3, is growth in exports of manufactured goods. Note that the *y*-axis scale of this graph and of the five component graphs of Figure 18-3 are the same size, enabling easy comparison.

(Source: Council of Economic Advisers, Economic Indicators, December 1991 and earlier.)

better! In fact, at the end of 1991, the U.S. trade balance excluding petroleum is nearly zero.

Does this mean that we should seek in panic to do without oil, as the popular lament goes today, or does it mean instead that we (like the Japanese!) are learning how to pay our own way in the trade arena—that we can pay for the imports we need with exports of our own manufacture. If we need oil, we buy it through exchange. If it is too expensive, we use less (conserve) and find substitutes. In principle, why should we do without products from elsewhere if we can pay for them with something of our own manufacture in trade?

If it is news to you that the U.S. trade balance at the end of 1991 was dramatically improving, then search through the graphs of the component economic sectors further, shown in Figure 18–3, looking for the key reason. The answer is that the big turnaround in the late 1980s and early 1990s has been the growth of U.S. exports of manufactured goods, excluding automobiles.

Does this support the idea that U.S. heavy industry is uncompetitive internationally? Does this support the idea that we should protect our manufacturing industries from foreign competition? Does this support the view that we should forsake the formation of international trading agreements meant to strengthen the development of other economies that will need new capital goods (from us)?

Even the balance of trade in automotive products is gradually improving. But does this mean that we should force a few more American cars into Japan and that all will then be well? What is so surprising about the fact that American cars, designed for the superhighways of a 3,000-mile-wide continental nation, should be less than desirable on a small, crowded island?

The turnaround in capital goods exports, as Federal Reserve

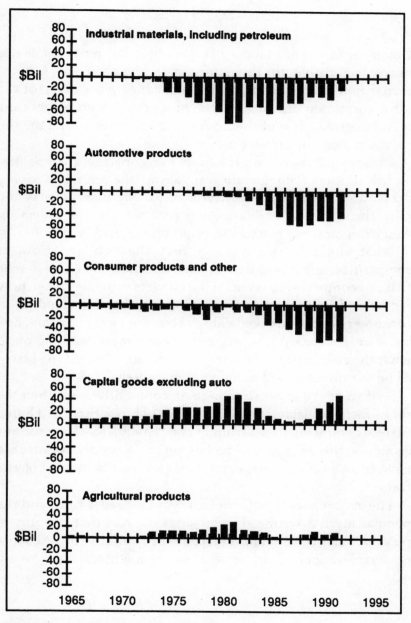

Figure 18-3. U.S. trade balance by sector.

Governor Lawrence Lindsey points out in his write-up, is not nearly so visible to the American citizen as the lack of turnaround in consumer goods (for instance, electronics) or the slow correction in automotive products. When Americans travel overseas, few of them tour foreign factories and see the new American machinery.

As more and more countries seek to reconstruct their politics in the image of democratic capitalism, the first big paying demand is for machinery with which to modernize industry and raise the standard of living—and so the trend for orders on American factories is likely to grow rather than wither.

What the facts point to is that the ebb and flow of competitiveness is mainly a matter of time. Thus, if it is true that our competitiveness in capital goods is returning, then how far behind in the same renovation will be our standing in consumer goods? Are we talking about the sweat of someone's brow in this regard (the work ethic) or simply catching on to what the customer really wants (wising up)? Should the blame all be put on labor and none on management?

So if trade is a guide to changes in competitiveness, then the set of facts available at the end of 1991 shows that the United States is bouncing back strongly and rapidly. If a vision for our economic future seems to be missing, it is mainly because we have focused on myths, emotions, and insults instead of the facts.

The lesson here is not whether Mr. Lindsey is right and the popular myth is wrong. The lesson is the role that skepticism plays in leading us along independent avenues toward more powerful outlooks than those of our competitors.

19

The Front Page and the Big Picture

In the present age, very little stays secret for long. Trends, even in their infancy, are reported on the front page. The difficulty is distinguishing the genuine from the myth, and in disentangling one's own desires for the future from what the future is most likely to be.

By *front page* I mean literally the front page of a single issue of a single paper. But I also mean the entire newspaper; I am talking about the collective body of information unleashed on civilization every day by thousands of printing presses in hundreds of countries. It is better for the executive to be content with what is on the front page than to yearn for all the details from all the pages in the universe of information. In an important sense, then, I am in disagreement with John Naisbitt, author of

Megatrends (see Chapter 12), who apparently has dozens of readers concentrating on hundreds of small-town newspapers, looking for new details. I would claim that what they find are new ideas rather than megatrends. But I would hasten to add that the new ideas are often quite interesting. Furthermore, the disagreement is easily solved: If you believe that Naisbitt's findings are important, simply add him to your own front page.

The front page is what you make it; it is what you believe contains coverage of the things of greatest importance to the broadest number of people, and thus eventually to business. Political events, at home and abroad, deserve the most prominent place on your front page. Politics is superior to economics; political ideas and conflicts will produce the main trends of interest to business.

Technology could itself be called a trend, but I am setting aside technology somewhat from the present discussion. What you do to follow technology is different from what you do to follow the *market* for technology. I am concerned with the market. Following the emergence of new technology for its technical essence requires a different method of monitoring—centering on research and development efforts, scanning the scientific literature, participating in government grants, attending scientific symposia, sponsoring university efforts, and so on.

POLITICAL AND CULTURAL TRENDS

Let's return to the political and cultural trends that will be the fabric for the markets of the future, whether involving old technology or new. The British writer George Orwell, who wrote *1984*, speaks about monitoring:

To see what is in front of one's nose needs a constant struggle. One thing that helps toward it is to keep a diary, or, at any rate, to keep some kind of record of one's opinions about important events. Otherwise, when some particularly absurd belief is exploded by events, one may simply forget that one ever held it. Political predictions are usually wrong, but even when one makes a correct one, to discover why one was right can be very illuminating. In general, one is only right when either wish or fear coincides with reality. If one recognizes this, one cannot, of course, get rid of one's subjective feelings, but one can to some extent insulate them from one's thinking and make predictions cold-bloodedly, by the book of arithmetic.[1]

In Chapter 13, I proposed that executives put their own forecasts of the main indicators in pencil at the bottom of their monthly updates and that they take time to assess their mistakes each month. This is a diary. This is the core of what is meant by monitoring. As Orwell suggests, however, the concept can be widened easily to include qualitative as well as quantitative elements. A notebook of clippings containing your own assessment of the front page of politics can be enormously useful, especially if you assign probabilities (Orwell's "book of arithmetic"). Look back over it periodically and give yourself an honest grade on how well you did forecasting trends.

You will fail when you confuse what you want to happen from what is happening. This very human tendency is a special problem for executives, because most will occasionally have to wear the hat of lobbyist as well as that of forecaster. A clear separation must be made. Nothing will decrease profits faster than aiming your assets at a trend you want rather than at one that is.

The key feature of monitoring the front page is seeing what is. If something is a myth, it should be so labeled. Much of what is on the front page is indeed myth. But people believe myths, so they play a massive role in the emergence of trends. The act of labeling a myth properly (which requires skepticism and irreverence) improves your ability to estimate its eventual impact and your ability to separate your own lobbying from your own forecasting.

Much of what appears on the front page about economics comes from experts who, whether they realize it or not, present a view of the way things *should* work in a free market. This, of course, ignores the reality of governments and politics. ("If things were as we would wish, then we would have our wishes.") A few years ago, I attended a conference that was addressed by the under secretary of agriculture. During the question and answer period, an economist chided the under secretary for not putting more stress on the overvalued dollar. The under secretary replied that the dollar was higher than we in agriculture would prefer it but that the dollar reflects economic reality. The questioner, undaunted, launched into a description of PPP (purchasing power parity), which he said we could use to calculate with certainty that the dollar is 30 percent overvalued. The under secretary shrugged and made no further comment. To me, and I think to the under secretary as well, that economist is simply missing what was on the front page. Reality is not obliged to conform with PPP theory, or any other theory. Neither are public officials.

The linguistic markers of theory and myth are euphemism, rhetoric, and cuteness. *Euphemism* is the substitution of an inoffensive term for one considered offensively explicit. For instance, instead of a White House press release saying, "A thousand men, women, and children were bombed with napalm," we might say, "A village was pacified." In a famous essay written in 1946 called "Politics and the English Language," George Orwell said:

> In our time, political speech and writing are largely the defense of the indefensible. Things like the continuance of British rule in India, the Russian purges and deportations, the dropping of the atom bombs on Japan, can indeed be defended, but only by arguments which are too brutal for most people to face, and which do not square with the professed aims of political parties. Thus political language has to consist largely of euphemism, question-begging and sheer cloudy vagueness.[2]

Orwell was reacting to his experience under BBC censors during the war, but his characterization of political language stands.

Rhetoric, as I am using the phrase, is unsupported or inflated discourse that usually attempts to make an emotional impact. For instance, someone who claims that the dollar is overvalued has an ax to grind; someone who says we have underinvested in high technology has a different kind of ax. And the person who appeals to parity is using a general concept to conceal a private formula that will perforce omit the factors that make reality *reality*.

In the March 1992 issue of *The Atlantic* (which in recent years has become a very good source of irreverent counteropinion), the lead article was entitled, "Jihad vs. McWorld: How the Planet Is Both Falling Apart and Coming Together—And What This Means for Democracy" (page 53). The author, Benjamin B. Barber, makes the case that market forces are causing the world to become more and more uniform, a condition he calls "McWorld," while on the other hand we see "Jihad, or the Lebonization of the World" going on. The juxtaposition of uniformity with diversity is good, but the language here is too cute. The language tips off that the author is perhaps not as concerned with clear, objective analysis as with the promulgation of a catchy concept that will make his idea popular.

Politics as reported on the front page will have lots of euphemism, rhetoric, and cuteness, and business reporting uses lots of economic jargon. Here is an example of the latter, taken from a *New York Times* article: "The economy rebounded smartly during the third quarter, and there are no signs that the nearly four-year expansion is about to expire, statistics to be published this week are expected to show."[3] As you can see, it is not enough to speculate on what all the numbers mean *after* they are published; we must do it beforehand. Once you have your own economic indicators coming to you in the form you want, are updating them routinely using officially released data, are making your own explicit forecasts, and are criticizing the forecasts' accuracy, you should skip articles such as the one above. In fact, you should skip nearly all interpretive articles. Stop reading them the moment you find economic jargon, unless the author, perhaps, is someone you regularly follow and respect, or unless you are venturing into a new area and simply need to develop context before you trust yourself.

Political news stories, with or without euphemism and rhetoric, deserve to be read, and read carefully. I often read the president's speeches until I think I know where he stands on issues of importance to my business, and I test my grasp by writing down what I believe he thinks, in plain English. I do the same when new pieces of legislation are introduced, until I grasp their structure; I do not follow every day's drama in Congress, usually, because the characters are too numerous. I mark clippings as I read, and label things as I see them— especially myths, rhetoric, and jargon.

As mentioned previously, the front page is what we choose to make it. It goes beyond the *New York Times* or whatever your main paper is. Your own front page is what you choose to make it, and it should have components from not only daily publications but from weekly, monthly, quarterly, and beyond. Weekly magazines such as *Time* and *Business Week* attempt to cover the principal trends affecting the consumer and business in a way that daily newspapers cannot. The same can be said of monthlies and quarterlies, especially in regard to scholarly publications. It is a good idea to have a few of these on your reading list, if only to illustrate the difference between what comes from the system of peer review and what comes from drama-driven journalists.

PERSONAL EXPERIENCE

Another part of the front page is your own attendance at various conferences and symposia. It may be that live gatherings are second only to newspapers for impact on us and for the instilling of new ideas. Executives who attend out-of-town conferences get away from their routines; they have climbed from their trenches and they have tacitly agreed to open themselves up to fresh new ideas. The conference organizers have gathered the best speakers they can find, the ones noted for stirring audiences. Even if the speaker is a scholar with hundreds of articles published, the peer review process renders that person much grander at a conference than in scholarly writing. The scholar thinks, "I've got to liven it up for the audience" and knows that no one is going to review the material before the speech. Thus the live conference has a way of becoming more of a political platform, for economists and others, than anything else on your front page. Keep this in mind as you take notes and later repeat to colleagues what you learned.

INFORMATION OVERLOAD

Much of what is on the front page will be followed by your competitors as well as by you—that is, the bulk of news has to be followed in a defensive manner. If you do not know about a new development and they do, you are at a disadvantage. This is another way of saying that we live in an age of information overload and that there is a minimum amount we must absorb to be viable. This does not mean, however, that we should try for maximum saturation. That would take us all the way back to intercepting every indicator that rolls off the government presses, which would require turning the intellectual process over to a team of people running a mathematical model. As I have said, such models will not produce as accurate a forecast as you can yourself, by means of a talented selection of what you read and a deliberate policy of what to exclude.

A cartoon in the *New Yorker* a few years ago showed a man in an easy chair watching television; on the screen was an announcer, using a pointer to show the four-digit number, 2,407. The caption read, "Today's number is two thousand four hundred and seven. That's sixteen above normal for this date and thirty-eight ahead of last month at this time." We hear so many numbers that we simply cannot know what they all mean—so there might as well be a number given that's just a number. Someone will find something to which it correlates nicely.

The point here is more than media overload. I have said earlier that the universe is complex, more complex than we think it is, more than we can imagine it to be. It has been this way always, even before the media blitz of the twentieth century. Life ceases if we do not simplify. And when following numbers we must simplify—carefully, but definitely.

Another article in the *New York Times* is also of interest. According to Professor A. Terry Bahill of the University of Arizona's Industrial Engineering Department:

> The big league fastball simply moves too fast for the eye to follow. By trying to keep his eye on the ball, even a keen-eyed batter will lose sight of it by the time it gets within five feet of the plate.... If a batter is to become a better hitter, he must train himself to occasionally take his eye off the ball in the middle of its trajectory, then voluntarily shift his field of vision closer to home plate and wait for the ball to arrive in that area.[4]

This situation is analogous to what I recommend about monitoring economic indicators, reading the front page of trends, and putting your view together in a single big picture. You need to implement deliberate systems, but you also need to break away from them. There is not a step-by-step formula that will work or a computerized routine that will take away the uncertainty. All you can do is face the next pitcher and do your best. What I am talking about in this book is a change of stance, perhaps, or of grip or focus, that I believe will add a few points to hitters who are already in the .300 range.

20

Plain Language—The Ultimate Resource

The language of business, in its written form, has come under enormous, mostly well-deserved, criticism in recent years. A full catalog of the alleged weaknesses—running from obscurity to pomposity—requires a lengthy lecture, and that is not my intent here. I want to address just one aspect of the problem, namely jargon, and I want to approach the subject first from a positive point of view. The good that jargon brings to business is often ignored by those giving the lectures.

The more efficient a business has become, I would argue, the more likely you are to find practitioners using lots of jargon. *Jargon* is the specialized or technical language of a trade or profession, or of a particular company. If a commodities broker says, "Sell ten Dec. corn," the order taker at the other end of the phone, perhaps on the floor of an exchange, knows exactly what to do. The two people can skip all the extra verbiage and use an agreed-upon code. It is efficient. Whenever business is faced with routine operations that are specialized and repetitive, jargon is invented automatically. It saves time and money.

But suppose the head commodities trader says to the chief executive, "We should dump out of this business—with the Fed pulling in and the dollar up, foreign economies will stay in the tank, loan rates will go down, our cash basis will stay narrow, and Chicago May–Dec. will never widen out. We can't make any money." The chief executive, if she came up through the ranks of traders, may believe she knows approximately what the head trader means, but in my opinion she should reject this kind of argument as no argument at all. As useful as jargon is in making daily operations efficient, it should have as little a role in strategic thinking as possible.

Strategic thinking is the most important function of the chief executive. Strategic thinking is the matching of assets with trends. The executive searches for the intersection of his company's abilities with his ideas about the future. The exercise is a time to be as free as possible from any kind of nonsense. It is a time to insist on clear, simple, plain language—and full context. No shortcuts. And at the same time, no elaborate pomposity.

Many textbooks of business prescribe a special language for strategic thinking with precise, special meanings suggested for such terms as *objectives, tactics, strengths and weaknesses,* and *strategies.* I believe that there can be no recipe for clear thinking; there can be only clear thinking. You cannot use a checklist to obtain easy results; you must invest the outright hard work of summoning up intellectual honesty (to the degree you have it) and applying it to the business operations of interest. The best recipe is a clean tablet. The best outcome is a statement in plain English—that is, no buzzwords. When it comes to strategic thinking, jargon obscures meaning, because jargon is stripped from the context you need to match internal operations with the external trends that will in the long run dominate profits.

Achieving clear language in business planning does not require an elaborate manual but rather a dedicated desire for it by the chief executive. People are capable of speaking and writing in clear prose if they are pushed to do so. The thrust is akin to the preceding chapter: If the leader adopts a new bearing in a need for assistance, there will emerge a group of assistants who find out how to provide what the executive needs. Those who are not accustomed to talking and writing in plain English—and certainly economists are frequently among such a group—will, when the executive consistently demands clarity instead of jargon, learn how to conform. Every community that has a major business will also have major resources in the humanities; local colleges and universities can be tapped for midnight instruction, if need be, on how to write clearly—at a very low cost compared with the payback that clarity provides to business strategy. Here is my central thesis: If you cannot explain something in simple language, you may not understand it yourself and other people will have difficulty understanding you.

More money is made and more competitors are beaten when all pretenses are dropped. Complexity of language is a clue that no one clearly understands the situation. Business situations, to be made profitable, must be grasped by a single mind—that of the chief executive. Grasp is increased as language is made simple, as context is expressed in plain words from ordinary speech. Jargon must be banished from strategic thinking.

Irreverence and skepticism should penetrate myths, so that underlying trends are as clear as they can be. You must rely on yourself, not on experts with models, to apprehend trends. Help is needed, but of a different kind than economists have been giving.

21

Analysis: The Right Kind and the Right Amount

If American business has been rightly accused of not paying appropriate attention to long-term results, it is a fault that stems in considerable degree from the fact that executives have virtually surrendered the function of forecasting to experts. Economics experts, in particular, apply elaborate methods to lots of data but achieve poor results.

Top management looks at how many millions are at stake and says, "Hire the best economists that money can buy and get the forecasts accurate. There are millions of dollars to be saved!" But when top management refuses to accept the responsibility for the inherent uncertainty of the firm's operation, many more millions are lost than saved.

And yet, experience shows that executives, as individuals and as teams, can and do improve their forecasting—if by no other means than by trying intelligently to do so.

The learning curve of forecasting accuracy is shown in Figure 21–1. The curve moves up sharply in the beginning, as expertise is first acquired. However, at some point, the curve flattens. Forecasts do not get better with more expertise; they get worse.

The secret to climbing the curve to the peak and staying there is to apply the right kind and the right amount of analysis. The right kind of analysis is that which fits the intellectual capacity, style, and singular experience of any particular executive. The right amount of analysis is equally hard to define with precision, but we do know what is too much. Analysis that involves hundreds of variables and removes the determination of causality from the mind itself, in favor of regression equations, is too much. Analysis that uses a few simple models to help explore and define causality, however, may be just right.

The concepts and methods presented in the final part of this book have been intended as a broad assortment from which any individual may pick and choose, and they may be added to the considerable array that any executive already possesses.

Accuracy. Complete accuracy is an unachievable intellectual ideal. In reality, knowledge of the world can only be approximate: We may attain a high probability of knowing where something is, and simultaneously its speed, but never a 100 percent probability.

But what kind of tolerances are we working with, and what is the best way to narrow them slightly, thereby beating competition? A well-organized company should expect to make annual forecasts slightly better than the plus or minus 10 percent error mentioned in Part One for projections of the entire economy, and it should expect to have fewer and smaller

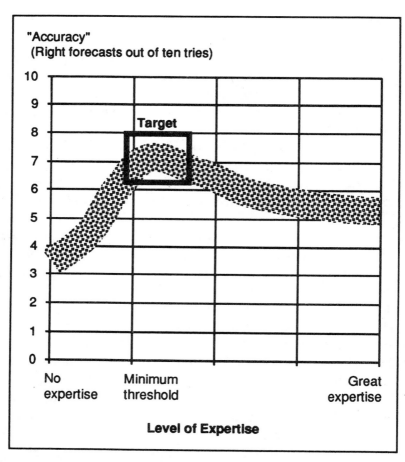

Figure 21-1. Forecast accuracy versus level of expertise.

Completely uniform forecasts by people with no expertise are usually much worse than those of the greatest experts. But executives who develop expertise to the minimum level can often beat the greatest experts.

(Source: Based on J. Scott Armstrong, How expert are the experts? Inc., December 1981.)

of the occasional large errors that occur when the fundamentals of the market change dramatically.

In terms of a quarterly or monthly forecast of sales, the following ranges and characterizations are possible:

5%	Impossible to maintain every month.
10%	Possible most of the time and credible with most managements.
15%	A general norm or average, but some managements may consider it "too sloppy."
20%	Bound to happen at least once or twice a year.
25%	Bad show. Forecaster did not see a wild card in time.

Feedback. One cannot approach forecasting successfully without a method, and yet every method that has ever been tried becomes a trap, sooner or later preventing its user from perceiving a new trend or a wild card before the competition sees it.

Instead I recommend independent thought and honest feedback on the results. This combination is nothing more than trying things until you find what works, and then carefully critiquing yourself after every forecast to pinpoint what went wrong and to learn something for the next round.

The big key is tracking the results and forcing the mind to see and accept its errors—after which it will find a better way to select, augment, display, and integrate the next time. Honest feedback is such hard work that few competitors will be willing to do it. Reviewing errors is terribly threatening to the relative positions of the people on the forecasting team.

Tracking Indicators. Executives should make a list of what they want to know about the economy and the format the list should have when it is done properly.

With the latest economic data at hand, organized to fit your own worldview, you put down your own forecasts of the future. You do this every time you get an updated table. Before you make a fresh forecast, however, you score how well you did on the last one. You check your projected figures against what the numbers actually became when released by the government. When you are wrong, you challenge your own arguments. Maybe you need to change the order of your factors, or maybe you are missing some factors that have now made themselves felt.

Correlations and Models. Correlations teach some important basic lessons in the structure of economic and business life. But the economist who systematically parses a hundred or a thousand data series will find lots of good correlations—but no strong predictability.

The way that economic indicators behave is like a family, or perhaps like a large herd of animals. Can you use the known position of one (or a few) animals in the herd to predict where the whole herd will be tomorrow? Or next week? Or a year from now?

A simple model that helps to make clear the interaction of a few key forces is good. The problem is with complex models that admit a multitude of forces and turn over the ownership of causality to a set of simultaneous equations. Since the user cannot clearly see how the forces are supposedly interacting, the user is left to trust that the mathematics have gotten it right—for which the only measure is how good the forecast is. And as we all know, when we put aside our wish that the method will work, econometric forecasts are a complete failure.

The best forecasts are made by the knowledgeable mind, assisted by regular tracking of the indicators and by live assessment of the overall environment in which economics and business are taking place.

Graphics. A proper grammar exists for graphing data, one that is never taught in universities and that is violated every day by many economists, journalists, and computer artists. The key idea is to maintain a consistent, preferably square framework throughout any analysis. Changing the framework of a graph is the same as changing the framework of the analysis. For instance, if you change the axis of a graph to magnify small changes, you must be prepared to own the importance you thus give to the magnification. You are adding the weight, not the data themselves.

The Domestic Business Cycle. Economists have produced dozens upon dozens of different models to explain the periodicity in the U.S. economy, with the hope of predicting the strength and timing of the next upturn or downturn. None of these methods have worked.

The technique I recommend is to adopt a common model of the cyle and track the data supporting the model in a way that makes its very ambiguity and inconclusiveness clear. The change in a set of supply-side and demand-side indicators can be displayed with a table of "yes's" and "no's." The principal message from the "yes–no" table is that the message is almost always a mixed message. This is not, in my view, a defect in the quality of the model, but a simple reflection of truth in today's complex reality. The world economy, with our domestic economy as a key constituent (sometimes leading, sometimes not), is under no universal obligation to behave in a neat and tidy fashion.

Bubble Charts. Ben Franklin's idea of "prudential algebra" can be applied to the weighting and analysis of your own personal economic forecasts. First, list all of the factors you believe will affect the economy in the coming period. Second, rank the factors by importance, on a scale from 0 to 10. Third, rate the factors according to their potential impact on the economy, either positive or negative. Fourth, combine the ranking and the rating into one single display, so that in Franklin's words, you have "got them all together in one view."

Irreverence and Skepticism. If the reader had to choose only one focus for his or her study of economic opinion and outlook, it should be the Fed. The Fed's view will not be right, but the Fed's view will certainly matter. This double insight is a key element of better forecasting. To beat our competition at forecasting, we must each become a better "Fed watcher" than our amateur counterparts in other companies.

It is not necessary to go public with one's irreverence, but it is necessary to have and exercise strong skepticism about economics news, commentary, and interpretation. Skepticism is the great virtue of the mind to take in what someone else says, hold it as possibly true, and then subject it to objective reasoning.

The Front Page. By *front page* I mean literally the front page of a single issue of a single paper. But I also mean the entire newspaper; I am talking about the collective body of information unleashed on civilization every day by thousands of printing presses in hundreds of countries.

The front page is what you make it; it is what you believe contains coverage of the things of greatest importance to the broadest number of people, and thus eventually to business. Political events, at home and abroad, deserve the most prominent place in your front page. Politics is superior to economics;

political ideas and conflicts will produce the main trends of interest to business.

As George Orwell said, "To see what is in front of one's nose needs a constant struggle." You will fail when you confuse what you want to happen from what is happening. This very human tendency is a special problem for executives, because most will occasionally have to wear the hat of lobbyist as well as that of forecaster. A clear separation must be made. Nothing will decrease profits faster than aiming your assets at a trend you want rather than at one that is.

Much of what is on the front page is indeed myth. But people believe myths, so myths play a massive role in the emergence of trends. The act of labeling a myth properly (which requires skepticism and irreverence) improves your ability to estimate its eventual impact and your ability to separate your own lobbying from your own forecasting.

Much of what appears on the front page about economics comes from experts who, whether they realize it or not, present a view of the way things should work in a free market.

Plain Language. Strategic thinking is the most important function of the chief executive. Strategic thinking is the matching of assets with trends. The executive searches for the intersection of the company's abilities with his or her ideas about the future. The exercise is a time to be as free as possible from any kind of nonsense. It is a time to insist on clear, simple, plain language—and full context. No shortcuts. And at the same time, no elaborate pomposity.

Achieving clear language in business planning does not require an intricate manual, but rather a dedicated desire for it by the chief executive. If you cannot explain something in simple language, you may not understand it yourself, and other people will surely have difficulty understanding you.

Notes

Chapter 2

1. John Eatwell, Murray Milgate, and Peter Newman, eds., *The New Palgrave, A Dictionary of Economics* (London: Macmillan, 1987).
2. Dennis Henderson, "Review of *The New Palgrave*," in *Blue Sheet, May 26, 1988* (Columbus: Department of Agricultural Economics and Rural Sociology, Ohio State University, 1988), 3.
3. Ibid., 4.
4. Quoted in Robert B. Reich, "Economics Can't Explain Everything," *Wall Street Journal*, 23 January 1989.

Chapter 3

1. *Federal Reserve Board Bulletin*, 3 July 1990.
2. David E. Rosenbaum, "Greenspan Sees No Cut in Rates Soon," *New York Times*, 19 July 1990.

3. *Federal Reserve Board Bulletin,* 24 July 1990.
4. "Fed Official's View," *New York Times,* 3 August 1990.
5. David Wessel and Rodney Ferguson, "Fed Says Economy Slowed Before Crisis," *Wall Street Journal,* 9 August 1990.
6. *Federal Reserve Board Bulletin,* 21 August 1990.
7. Martin Rosenberg, "Recession Risk High, But Not Certain, Fed Official Says," *Kansas City Star,* 14 September 1990.
8. Federal Reserve Board press release of testimony by Alan Greenspan, 19 September 1990.
9. *Federal Reserve Board Bulletin,* 2 October 1990.
10. *Federal Reserve Board Beige Book,* 19 October 1990.
11. *Federal Reserve Board Bulletin,* 13 November 1990.
12. Federal Reserve Board press release of testimony by Alan Greenspan, 20 November 1990.
13. *Federal Reserve Board Bulletin,* 18 December 1990.
14. Lindley H. Clark, Jr., "Has the Long-Awaited Recession Arrived?" *Wall Street Journal,* 13 August 1990.
15. Alan Murray and David Wessel, "Brady Sees Rise in Oil Prices Cutting Growth," *Wall Street Journal,* 13 August 1990.
16. "Disagreeing about the Consensus," *The Economist,* 27 July 1991.
17. Ibid.

Chapter 4

1. Peter Passell, "Economics Nobel to a Basic Thinker," *New York Times,* 16 October 1991; and Michael Prowse, "Realist Wins Nobel Prize for Economics," *Financial Times,* 16 October 1991.
2. Passell, "Economics Nobel."
3. Prowse, "Realist Wins."
4. Dennis L. Meadows et al., *The Limits of Growth* (New York: Universe Books, 1972).
5. Peter F. Drucker, "The Changed World Economy," *Foreign Affairs,* Spring 1986, 768–791.
6. Edward Cowan, "U.S. Revising GNP of 1977, Adds 3% Growth," *New York Times,* 21 July 1984.

7. U.S. Department of Commerce, *Survey of Current Business*, various issues.
8. Henry Kaufman, "Kaufman Says 'Orthodoxy of Monetarism' Will Probably Be Replaced," *Commodity News Service*, 6 June 1985.

Chapter 6

1. John Henry Newman, *An Essay in Aid of a Grammar of Assent* (London: Longmans, Green & Co., 1924), 360–361.
2. Newman, *An Essay*, 361.

Chapter 8

1. Dan Dorfman, "With Failure of the Pros, What's a Private Investor to Do?" *Chicago Tribune*, 21 October 1984.
2. "Oil Prices: Living with the Perils of Prophecy," *Petroleum Intelligence Weekly*, 3 December 1984, 7.
3. John Kenneth Galbraith, *Economics in Perspective* (Boston: Houghton Mifflin, 1987), 264.

Chapter 9

1. Michael E. Porter, *Competitive Strategy* (New York: The Free Press, 1980).
2. Michael E. Porter, *Competitive Advantage* (New York: The Free Press, 1985).

Chapter 12

1. John Naisbitt, *Megatrends: Ten New Directions Transforming Our Lives* (New York: Warner Books, 1982).

Chapter 16

1. Michael Lehman, *The Down Jones-Irwin Guide to Using the Wall Street Journal* (Homewood, IL: Dow Jones-Irwin, 1984).

Chapter 17

1. Quoted in Robyn M. Dawes, "Forecasting One's Own Preference," *International Journal of Forecasting* 2, no. 5 (1986); 5.

Chapter 18

1. Lawrence B. Lindsey, "America's Growing Economic Lead," *Wall Street Journal*, 7 February 1992.

Chapter 19

1. George Orwell, "In Front of Your Nose," in *The Collected Essays, Journalism and Letters of George Orwell*, vol. 4, ed. Soma Orwell and Ian Angus (New York: Harcourt Brace Jovanovich, 1968), 125.
2. George Orwell, "Politics and the English Language," in *The Collected Essays*, 127–140.
3. Michael Quint, "Economy Gives Alternating Signals," *New York Times*, 14 October 1985.
4. A. Terry Bahill, "Take Your Eye Off the Ball, Scientist Coaches Sluggers," *New York Times*, 12 June 1984.

Index